BUSINESS CONTACTS

Other Business English Titles

BRIEGER, N. and J. COMFORT
Business Issues

DUNLOP, I. and H. SCHRAND
Communication for Business

FITZPATRICK, A.
*English for International Conferences**

McGOVERN, J. and J. McGOVERN
*Bank On Your English**

McKELLEN, J. and M. SPOONER
*New Business Matters**

PALSTRA, R.
*Telephone English**

POTE, M. et al
*A Case for Business English**

* includes audio cassettes

BUSINESS CONTACTS

Materials for developing listening and speaking skills for the student of Business English

N. Brieger, J. Comfort, S. Hughes,
C. West

ENGLISH LANGUAGE TEACHING

Prentice-Hall International

New York London Toronto Sydney Tokyo Singapore

First published 1987 by
Prentice Hall International (UK) Ltd,
66 Wod Lane End, Hemel Hempstead,
Hertfordshire, HP2 4RG
A division of
Simon & Schuster International Group

© 1987 Prentice Hall International (UK) Ltd

All rights reserved. No part of this publication may be reproduced, stored in a retrieval system, or transmitted, in any form, or by any means, electronic, mechanical, photocopying, recording or otherwise, without the prior permission, in writing, from the publisher.
For permission within the United States of America contact Prentice Hall Inc., Englewood Cliffs, NJ 07632.

Printed and bound in Great Britain by
BPCC Wheatons Ltd, Exeter

Library of Congress Catalog Card No: 83-25005

British Library Cataloguing in Publication Data

Business contacts. – (Materials for language practice)
1. English language – Text-books for foreign speakers
2. English language – Business English
I. Brieger, N. II. Series
428.2'4'02465   PE1128

ISBN 0-13-093311-2

Dedicated to

STEVE HUGHES

With acknowledgements to colleagues at York Language Training Associates for encouragement and advice

Introduction

Rationale

In recent years materials writers seem to have aligned themselves with a single methodological approach – either grammatical, notional/functional or situational. In the light of the claims made in support of each of them, we have felt free to follow an eclectic approach and have simply used the approach which we felt was most suitable for presenting each of the language areas.

In response to the need for materials which can be used both by the learner on his own and by the group teacher we have attempted to strike a balance between controlled exercises and open-ended activities.

These materials are aimed at students who have a professional need for English in commercial/industrial fields: people either in, or training for, top, middle or lower management posts, or personal assistants, secretaries, sales representatives, etc. They can be used in conjunction with either a business English course or a general English course.

More specifically, this listening-based material is relevant for learners who need either revisionary or supplementary communicative practice around:

1. key functional areas (Units 1 – 10);
2. key grammatical areas (Units 11 – 19);
3. key notional areas (Units 20 – 30).

The materials are designed to develop the listening skills of:

1. extracting relevant information;
2. structuring information;
3. inferring meaning from context;
4. becoming accustomed to different varieties of English (formal and informal).

The materials also develop oral production skills around:

1. discussion topics;
2. role plays;
3. problem solving activities.

Organisation of material

Each unit consists of:

1. **Listening**
   A short taped listening comprehension passage, accompanied by an information transfer exercise.
2. **Presentation**
   Highlighting and explanation of language items from the listening comprehension passage.
3. **Controlled Practice**
   An exercise or exercises designed to practise the language items introduced in the presentation.
4. **Transfer**
   Pair work or group work designed to encourage students to use the language introduced in the presentation in a business-oriented context.

In the second part of the book is a Key Section for each unit which contains:

1. **Listening**
   A tapescript and answers to the information transfer exercise.
2. **Controlled Practice**
   Answers to the controlled practice exercise(s).
3. **Transfer** (where necessary)
   Information for pair work activities.

The **Glossary** at the back of the book provides explanation and examples of the use of important business related vocabulary from the taped passages.

The roles of the teacher and the students

The materials provide the teacher with an opportunity to strike a balance between two classroom roles, teacher-controlled and teacher-monitored.

They also give students an opportunity for autonomous learning (via self-access).
Sections 1, 2, and 3 (Listening, Presentation and Controlled Practice) can be done with or without a teacher.
Section 4 (Transfer) can be done by student groups or pairs without a teacher, although in many of the units some form of teacher monitoring is advisable.

Suggested additional reference material

1 An appropriate dictionary – to enable the student to exploit fully the vocabulary introduced in the units.

2 A communicative grammar – to enable the student to reinforce and expand upon the form and function of the language presented.

Teachers' Notes

Uses of material

i   As supplementary material to a General English Course, where students have an interest in or a need for business English.
ii As supplementary material to a Business English Course.
iii As extensive course material for English component in Business or Management Training Course.
iv As a self-study/homework component for a Business English Course. (The Transfer section can be used for classroom follow-up.)
v   As follow-up material on completion of a course.

Selection of material

i   According to 'Topic' (See Contents page).
ii According to 'Language Area' (See Contents page).

The units can either provide further practice in a language area or present a language area for the first time.

Unit handling

The first three sections of each unit can be done without a teacher present.

1 Listening
i   Introduce the students to the listening passage.
ii Prepare the students for the listening task/activity by teaching any unfamiliar vocabulary and explaining the task if necessary.
iii Play tape right through, without stopping.
iv Play tape again, if necessary. (This time, the students may be allowed to listen at their own pace.)
v   Let students check their answers with the Key.
vi Play tape a third time if there are major differences between the Key and student answers.
vii Refer students to the Glossary for vocabulary problems.

2 Presentation
i   Ask students to read through the presentation and explanation of the language area.
ii Help students with unknown vocabulary.

3 Controlled Practice
i   Ask students to complete the exercise(s) and then to check their answers with the Key.
ii Advise on alternative answers or give revisionary practice where appropriate.

4 Transfer
The activities in this section are designed to give students free practice in the use of the language which has been presented in the unit. The activities are either pair work or group work.

PAIR WORK
i   Divide the class into pairs.
ii In most cases these activities involve students in information exchange. Where this is the case, part of the information is in the Key Section at the back of the book and one student should turn to that section. This is marked clearly in the text.
iii Make sure that each student looks only at one set of information.
iv Monitor the pairs as they carry out the transfer activity, prompting the use of the practised language if necessary.

GROUP WORK
i   The class may be kept as one unit for these activities or divided into smaller groups.
ii Monitor, chair and, if necessary, prompt discussion.
iii Encourage students to make use of the language they have been introduced to in the unit.

Try not to interrupt too much at this stage in the lesson but make notes of the proceedings and spend some time on a remedial or revisionary session after the transfer activity is completed.

Notes to the Student

This material is designed for students who have some previous knowledge of English and wish to revise their language or re-apply it in a business context. It can be used by students working alone; as self-study or homework material during a course; or as follow-up material on completion of a course.

Selection of material

You can, of course, simply work through the materials as they are presented in the book. Alternatively you may choose a unit on the basis of topic or language area (see contents page). The topic areas listed indicate the themes of the listening passages and related transfer exercises.

There are three main language areas:
i Functional 10 units giving practice in performing key language activities like giving opinions, agreeing and disagreeing, making introductions, etc.
ii Grammatical 9 units dealing with common problem areas like tense usage, conditionals, frequency adverbs, etc.
iii Notional 11 units giving practice in language concept areas like comparison and contrast, sequence, plans and intentions etc.

If you feel, therefore, that you have a particular weakness in any of these areas you can choose a unit which will give you practice in that area.

Using a unit

The first three sections of each unit can be done without a teacher. For the last section (Transfer) you need at least one other student to work with you and you may require the help of a teacher.

1 Listening
The listening activities are of 4 main kinds:
a recording information which you hear on the tape onto a table or diagram in your book;
b saying whether statements about the passage you have heard are true or false;
c recording the opinions or attitudes of speakers you hear on the tape;
d making brief notes about information which you hear on the tape.

In each case the exercise is intended to help you listen more actively. The following procedure is suggested for the most effective use of the listening section.
i Read the introduction to Listening and make sure that you understand the task or activity before you listen to the tape.
ii Listen to the tape without stopping it.
iii As you listen, or after you have listened, complete the task.
iv If necessary, listen again. This time stop the tape and replay sections if you need to.
v Check your answers with the Key. If your answers are wrong, listen again to the tape and try to see why you made mistakes.
vi Use the Glossary if you cannot understand some of the words.

2 Presentation
i Read carefully the presentation and explanation of the language area.
ii Try to remember how this language was used on the tape. If you want, play the tape again.

3 Controlled Practice
i Complete the exercise(s).
ii Check your answers with the Key.
iii If your answers are wrong, look again at the Presentation and try to see why you have made mistakes.

4 Transfer
Pair Work
i Choose a fellow student, friend etc.
ii Decide who is Student A and who is Student B.

iii Student A should *only* look at Student A copy.
iv Student B should *only* look at Student B copy in the Key Section.
v Carry out the transfer activity. Try to use the language you have learnt in the unit.

Group Work
This is best carried out in a class.

Contents

The contents list below indicates the topic themes of the taped passage for each unit and the language area covered in that unit. Units 1 – 10 are functional units, units 11 – 19 grammatical and units 20 – 30 notional.

Unit 1	Greeting friends and strangers *Introductions and greetings*		Unit 16	Interview preparations *Defining relative clauses*
Unit 2	Requesting travel information *Asking for information*		Unit 17	Sales call *Asking questions*
Unit 3	Arranging accommodation *Telephone language*		Unit 18	Office talk (2) *Present perfect tense*
Unit 4	Checking information *Checking and correcting*		Unit 19	Office talk (3) *Present perfect v past simple tenses*
Unit 5	Requesting action *Requesting action, thanking, apologising*		Unit 20	Past appointments, future engagements *Time reference*
Unit 6	Reviewing the interviewees *Expressing likes, dislikes, preferences*		Unit 21	Making arrangements *Plans and intentions*
Unit 7	Allocating the budget *Agreeing and disagreeing*		Unit 22	Recruitment procedures *Sequencing*
Unit 8	Management qualities *Giving opinions*		Unit 23	Deciding company policy *Obligation*
Unit 9	Pricing policy *Making suggestions*		Unit 24	Product description *Dimension and size*
Unit 10	Office talk (1) *Requesting, granting, refusing permission*		Unit 25	Value, price and efficiency *Value and price*
Unit 11	Wages and prices *Present simple and present progressive tenses*		Unit 26	Inflation *Describing graphs*
Unit 12	Travel expenses *Past simple tense*		Unit 27	Delivery dates *Prediction and certainty*
Unit 13	Work routines *Expressions of frequency*		Unit 28	Sales *Similarity and difference*
Unit 14	Company rules and regulations *Modal verbs*		Unit 29	Market share developments *Comparison and contrast*
Unit 15	Plans and strategies *Conditional sentences (I and II)*		Unit 30	End of year report *Definite quantity and amount*

The Key Section, containing tapescripts, answers and additional information, begins on page 76.

Unit 1 Greeting friends and strangers

1 Listening

Listen to the tape on which you will hear people being introduced, introducing themselves and greeting each other. As you listen, match the names of the people who are being introduced, introducing themselves and greeting each other. (The first names have already been matched.)

Now listen again and indicate in the left-hand column whether the introduction is 'formal' (F) or 'informal' (I). (The first one has been done for you.)

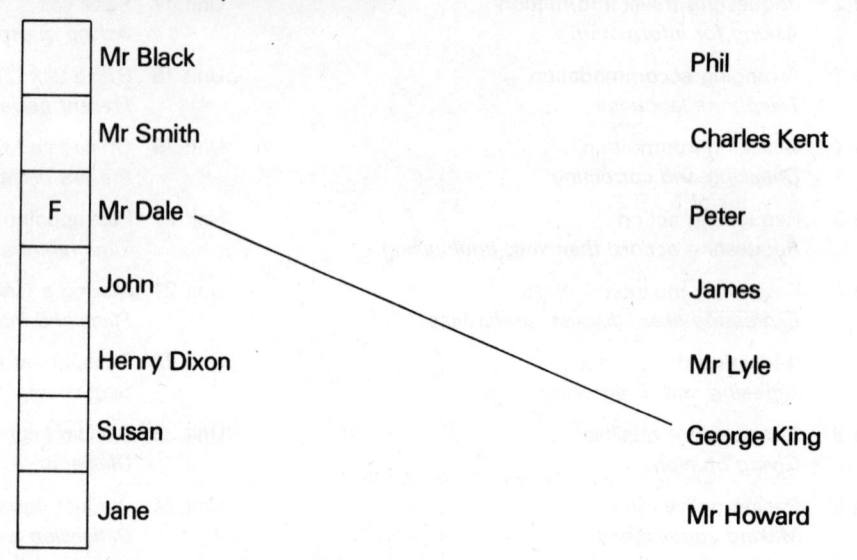

	Mr Black	Phil
	Mr Smith	Charles Kent
F	Mr Dale	Peter
	John	James
	Henry Dixon	Mr Lyle
	Susan	George King
	Jane	Mr Howard

(Mr Dale is matched with George King.)

2 Presentation

Here is some of the language you have just heard.

INTRODUCING SOMEONE ELSE

Formal: I'd like to introduce you to Mr...
Pleased to meet you, my name's...
or
Let me introduce you two. Mr..., this is Mr...

Informal: Jill, this is Richard.
Nice to meet you, ...

INTRODUCING YOURSELF

Formal: How do you do, I'm John Smith.
How do you do. My name's Brown, Neil Brown.

Informal: Hello, my name's Chris.
Nice to meet you. Mine's Jenny.

GREETING SOMEBODY

Formal: Good morning. Mr Sloane. How are you?
Very well, thank you, Mr Jones. I hope you are well too.

Informal: Hello, Dick. How are you?
I'm fine. What about you? (or And you?)

8

3 Controlled Practice

Complete the dialogues.

1 Introducing a business colleague to a customer
'_____ to introduce you to Mr Kline.'
'Pleased to meet you, _____ Harvey, Joseph Harvey.'

2 Introducing a friend to a friend
'Mary, _____ Mark.'
'_____.'

3 Introducing yourself to the director of a subsidiary company
'_____, I'm Graham Stanton, finance manager of GAB Ltd.'
'_____, my name's Clark, I'm the director of GAB France.'

4 Introducing yourself to someone you would like to dance with at a party
'_____, my name's Chris.'
'Hello, _____ Sarah.'

5 Greeting a friend for the first time in the day
'Hello, Max. _____?'
'I'm fine. _____?'

6 Greeting your boss when you meet him in the lift in the afternoon
'_____, Mr Ross. How are you?'
'Very well thank you. _____, Mr Stanton.'

7 Introducing a client to a colleague
'Let me _____ Mr Carne, _____ Mr Saxon, a colleague of mine.'

4 Transfer

GROUP WORK

Work in groups of three.
Each member of the group should introduce him/herself, introduce the other two members of the group and greet the other two members of the group in the following situations:
i at a formal cocktail party;
ii at a friendly late evening party.

Unit 2

Requesting travel information

1 Listening

Listen to the dialogue in which one person is requesting information from another. The dialogue takes place in a travel office. As you listen note down briefly the information requested. There are six pieces of information.

1 _____
2 _____
3 _____
4 _____
5 _____
6 _____

2 Presentation

Here is some of the language you have just heard for requesting information.
Could you tell me...?
Can you tell me...?
Do you happen to know...?
I wonder if you'd let me know...
I wonder if you'd tell me...

Notice how the above phrases are followed.
Can you tell me *when the first flight to Hamburg is*?
NB In a direct question When is the first flight to Hamburg?
Do you happen to know *if the flight is fully booked*?
NB In a direct question Is the flight fully booked?

These indirect question forms generally sound more polite than the direct form and are, therefore, particularly suitable when asking for information from a person you do not know.

3 Controlled Practice

Change the following direct questions into polite requests for information. You can use any of the phrases presented above.

1 What time does the first plane leave for Paris?
_____

2 Are the hotels cheaper in Birmingham than in London?
_____

3 What is the best way to travel from London to York?
_____

4 Is there a seat available on the 2.30 flight?
_____

5 How much does a first class ticket to Edinburgh cost?
_____

6 Did the airline company recently increase its prices?
_____

7 Do I have to change at Manchester?
_____

8 Which airport does the plane leave from?
_____

9 Why are there no flights on Sunday?
_____

10 Is the plane going to be delayed because of the fog?
_____

4 Transfer

PAIR WORK

Student A
Ask your partner for the following information about car hire facilities.

Student A copy

Information areas		
	1	Models available
	2	Basic hire charge
	3	Mileage charge
	4	Insurance charge
	5	Other charges
	6	Minimum hire time

Student B
Use the table in the Key Section to give appropriate information to your partner's questions.

Unit 3 Arranging accommodation

1 Listening

Listen to the tape on which Jane Stevens, the Personal Assistant to the Managing Director of Daxia, is making accommodation arrangements for three foreign visitors. They are coming to Daxia next week to attend a conference.

On the tape you will hear her telephone three hotels. As you listen, fill in the information in the table provided. (In some cases a tick or a cross will do; in others you will have to write a few words.)

	Hotel 1	Hotel 2	Hotel 3
Name of hotel			
Location			
Noisy/ quiet			
Restaurant			
Bar			
Dancing			
Sauna			
Swimming pool			

Below are the preferences of the three foreign visitors. In which hotel would you put each of them?

Jean Mason	Enrico Marietti	Claude Leclerc
quiet countryside keeping fit	good food and drink socialising entertainment	theatre/cinema talking business eating out

2 Presentation

Here is some of the language you have just heard.

Notice how certain features are common to most telephone calls.

1 Answer
Leeds 43267.
Midland Hotel. Can I help you?
Paul Renolds speaking/Renolds here.

2 Greetings
Good morning/afternoon/evening.
Hello. (informal)

3 Topics
a Caller's introduction
My name is...
I'm...from Marbella Properties Ltd.
This is....
b Caller's request for connection
Could I speak to Mr..., please?
Could you put me through to the Sales Department, please?
Could I have Accounts, please?
The Production Department, please.
c Response
One moment, please.
Could you hang on a minute, please.
Trying to connect you.
Putting you through now.
I'm afraid he's not in at the moment. Would you like to leave a message?
d Request for information
I wonder if you could tell me...
I'm ringing to find out about...
The reason I've called is to ask you...

4 Pre-closing sequence
Well, thanks very much for the information.
Thanks for your help.
It was very nice talking to you.
Look forward to hearing from you again soon.
See you next week, then.

5 Closing greetings
Bye.
See you. (informal)

3 Controlled Practice

Below is a jumbled telephone conversation in which Paul Peters (B) rings Mr Bramhall (C) of Smiths Components to find out about the delivery of some goods he had ordered. But first Mr Peters speaks to the receptionist (A).

Can you arrange the sentences in the right order below?

B No, I'll hang on.
B Good morning. This is Paul Peters from Spracken Spares.
C Dispatch Section.
A Smiths Components.
A I'm sorry. Who did you want to speak to?
B I'm phoning to find out about the delivery of the X428's we ordered last week.
B Good. That's what I hoped you'd say. Thank you. Bye.
B Mr Bramhall in the Dispatch Section.
B Good morning. This is Paul Peters of Spracken Spares. Could I speak to Mr Bramhall in the Dispatch Section?
C Good morning, Mr Peters. What can I do for you?
B Hello. Is that Mr Bramhall?
C Bye.
C Well, I've just this minute dispatched them to you and they should arrive this afternoon.
C Yes, speaking.
A One moment, please.
   I'm afraid he's on the phone at the moment. Could you hold on a minute or would you rather leave a message?

---

4 Transfer

PAIR WORK

The following transfer activities are telephone simulations and are best practised with a telephone bug.

A Asking for information

Student A
Ring up the Mercantile Bank.
Ask to be put through to the foreign section.
Find out about the buying and selling rate for:
US Dollars
£ Sterling
German Marks
French Francs

Student B
Answer the phone using the information in the Key Section for this unit.

B Complaining

Student A
You have just returned from a holiday in Lagunda. Unfortunately the holiday was spoiled because the hotel rooms were dirty, the hotel was very noisy and the food was atrocious.

You feel that the travel agent should refund you some of the money.
Telephone him and make your complaints tactfully.

Student B
Answer the call using the information given in the Key Section.

Now change roles if you have time.

Unit 4 Checking information

1 Listening

A Listen to the first three dialogues in which someone makes a mistake. For example, he or she gives someone the wrong name or the wrong information.

As you listen, tick the box beside the correct name or information.

Dialogue 1 The visitor's name was

Liddle	
Little	

Dialogue 2 The company is looking for

a junior clerk	
a senior clerk	

Dialogue 3 The company

can offer the young man a job	
cannot offer him a job	

B Listen to the next two dialogues in which important information is given and the listener wants to make sure he has heard it correctly.

As you listen, write down the correct information in the boxes below.
Dialogue 4 Write down the caller's name

_____

_____

Dialogue 5 Write down
i the amount on the bill

_____

ii the amount the caller thinks he owes

_____

_____

iii the invoice number

_____

2 Presentation

A CORRECTING WRONG NAMES, INFORMATION
Here is some of the language you heard in the first three dialogues. Notice how it is used to correct mistakes.

Excuse me. Not Little – *Liddle*. (The correct word is emphasised.)

That's not quite right.

I'm afraid you/Mr X etc. made a mistake. (The correct information is given.)

Listen to the tape again and notice the way these phrases are spoken. Which words are emphasised? Underline them on your tapescript in the Key Section.

B CHECKING INFORMATION
Here is some of the language you have heard in dialogues 4 and 5.

There are several ways to check that you have heard or understood information correctly. These are:
i repeating the information (often with a rising intonation like a question)
ii repeating the first part of the information so that the person giving the information has to complete it
iii asking for repetition
Can (or Could...) you repeat that please?
Can you spell that please?
iv stating that you did not hear correctly
Sorry, I didn't quite catch that/your name/your invoice number.

Listen to the last two dialogues again. Listen to the intonation of the phrases given here. Notice which words are emphasised and mark them on your tapescript.

3 Controlled Practice

A The statements below all contain a mistake. Correct them using one of the phrases from the Presentation and the correction given in the brackets.

example: The time in Dubai is four hours *behind* Greenwich Mean Time. (ahead of)
That's not right. The time in Dubai is four hours *ahead of* Greenwich Mean Time.

1 The time in New York is *seven* hours behind Greenwich Mean Time. (four hours)

2 *Sweden* has many oilfields in the North Sea. (Norway)

3 Concord flies from France to *Argentina*. (Brazil)

4 Marseilles is the biggest port in the *North of Spain*. (South of France.)

5 *Spanish* is the national language of Brazil. (Portuguese)

6 Tahiti is an island in the *Indian* Ocean. (Pacific)

7 The lira is the currency of *Spain*. (Italy)

8 Lombard Street is the centre of English *insurance*. (banking)

B Listen to the next section on the tape. You will hear ten items of information. After each item there will be a pause on the tape. Practise using the phrases given in the Presentation for checking information. If you hear a name, ask for the spelling; ask for numbers to be repeated, and so on. You will then hear the main part of the information repeated. Write down what you hear and then check it with the Key.

4 Transfer

Student A
Look at information sheet A below.

Student B
Look at information sheet B in the Key Section.
Look only at your own information sheet.

You each have a list of facts and figures about Mexico, giving information about the area, population, industries etc. Information sheet A is the correct copy. B contains 10 mistakes. Find the mistakes by checking each item of information. Student A may begin by reading the first item (area) while B checks it with his figure, using one of the ways practised for checking information. If B's figure differs from A's, A should give the correct information from his sheet. Note down the mistake and then continue. B may read the second item, and A check it and so on.

When you have found all the mistakes, report back to the rest of the class.

Information Sheet A

MEXICO Facts and Figures

Area 1 967 183 square kilometres

Population (1970) 48 377 363

Geography mountainous with desert in the West.

Politics Mexico is a federal republic. There are 31 states and the district of Mexico City.

Economy the most important exports are cotton, sisal, sulphur, silver, oil.

Industries there are several large oil refineries and a petrochemical complex at Cosoleacaque; tourism is also important and there is a rapidly expanding consumer goods industry.

Mexico City the capital of Mexico and the largest city in central and southern America.
altitude: 2278 metres
population: (1970) circa 6 874 165
climate: average maximum temperature 18.3 C. (May)
average minimum temperature 11.9 C. (December)
average rainfall 587 millimetres per year — wet in summer, dry in winter.

Unit 5 Requesting action

1 Listening

Listen to the dialogue, in which Mr Jackson telephones his secretary, Helen, and asks her to do several things. Mr Jackson is in Hong Kong on business. His secretary is in England.

Now answer the questions. Write your answers in the spaces provided.

What does Mr Jackson ask Helen to do?	Can she do them right away?
1	Yes/No
2	Yes/No
3	Yes/No
4	Yes/No

2 Presentation

Here is some of the language you have just heard. Notice the different ways to make requests, and ways of responding.

After reading through the phrases, play the tape again and listen to the way they are used.

Making Requests

Responses

	You can't do it	You can do it
Can you find File No. 125/cif, please? Could you copy the contents of the file? Would you do that right away, please? Would you mind doing it in the morning?	I'm sorry; I can't. That's not possible, I'm afraid.	Yes, of course. Certainly. I'll do it right away.

You can also apologise like this	Responses
I'm terribly sorry. I'm so sorry.	It's quite all right. Never mind.

When the requested action is completed, you should thank the other person

Thank you very much (or so much).

I'm very grateful to you.

NB *Would you mind...* is always followed by ...*ing*.

e.g. Would you mind open*ing* the window?

3 Controlled Practice

A The following can sound very impolite. Make them into polite requests. Use the phrases given in the Presentation above.

1 Speak up – I can't hear you.
2 Say that again – I didn't understand.
3 Lend me your pen.
4 Tell me where the canteen is.
5 Send a telex to confirm that.
6 Let me know what happens.
7 Phone me back in half an hour.
8 Drive me to the station.
9 Pass me the telephone directory.
10 Give me some change for the telephone.

B Request each of the following actions to be carried out. How would you respond to the requests?

e.g. Request Would you please book a return ticket to Paris for me, leaving Sunday?
Response Yes, of course.
/I'm sorry. I can't. (There are no flights to Paris on Sunday.)

1 Book a return ticket to Paris for me, leaving Sunday.
2 Reserve a room for me at the Meridian Hotel for Thursday and Friday.
3 Get two tickets for the theatre for Saturday night.
4 Phone the office and tell them I'll be late.
5 Tell Mr James I'd like to see him.
6 Fetch me a train timetable.
7 Make a photocopy of this document.
8 Go and see if Mr Philips has arrived yet.
9 Bring some more letter paper.
10 Empty the waste paper basket.

4 Transfer

PAIR WORK

Student A
It is Monday. You are sick and will be absent from the office for the whole week. Phone and ask your colleague, Student B, to carry out the activities you had planned for the week in your diary below.

Student B
Look at your schedule in the Key Section and respond to Student A's requests.

Mon	am	brief sales team
	pm	meeting with Development, 2.30
Tues	am	attend demonstration of new product, Nottingham
	pm	feedback session on demonstration
Wed	am	
	pm	correspondence
Thurs	am	check need for immediate follow-up to last week's mailing
	pm	meeting with Production Dept. 2.15
Fri	am	lunch with Board of Trade rep.
	pm	sales team report back

Unit 6 Reviewing the interviewees

1 Listening

Listen to the discussion about three candidates – Brown, Smith and Jones – who have just been interviewed for a job by a panel. The panel consists of three people – John, who speaks first, then Peter and finally Susan.

As you listen, indicate which candidate is liked (put a ✓), which candidate is disliked (put a ✗) and which candidate is preferred by the three members of the panel (put a ✱).

	Mr Brown	Mr Smith	Mr Jones
John			
Peter			
Susan			

2 Presentation

Here is some of the language you have just heard.

Notice how it is used to express likes, dislikes and preferences.

LIKES

I *liked* Mr Jones.
I *enjoy* interviewing. (Normally, we enjoy something, not somebody.)
I *was keen on* offering the job to Mr Jones.

DISLIKES

I *didn't like* Mr Brown (or I *disliked* Mr Brown).
NB *disliked* is stronger than *didn't like*.
I *hate* interviewing.
I *can't stand* people like him.

PREFERENCES

I *preferred* Smith *to* Jones. I'd *prefer to* offer the job to Mr Smith.
I'd *rather* he got the job *than* Smith. I'd *rather* offer the job to Mr Jones.

NB I'd rather... = I would rather...
    I'd prefer to... = I would prefer to...

3 Controlled Practice

Look at the results below of a rail survey in which daily commuters between Earswick and the capital were asked the following three questions:

1 Do you like travelling by train?

2 If not, how would you prefer to travel?

3 Is there any way you would not like to travel?

Question 1	YES 55% NO 45%
Question 2	In own car 40%
	In company car 42%
	As car passenger 12%
	By bus 6%
Question 3	By bus 25%
	In own car 33%
	As car passenger 32%
	In company car 10%

Now use the information above to complete the following sentences:

1 55% _____
travelling by train.

2 45% _____
travelling by train.

3 40% _____
to travel in their own car.

4 25% _____
to travel by bus.

5 42% _____
travel in a company car.

6 12% _____
to travel as a car passenger.

7 6% _____
travel by bus than by train.

8 33% _____
to travel in their own car.

9 32% _____
to travel as a car passenger.

10 10% _____
to travel in a company car.

4 Transfer

GROUP WORK

Carry out a similar survey to the one opposite amongst your group.

1 Ask questions about travelling likes, dislikes and preferences.

2 Tabulate the results.

Unit 7 Allocating the budget

1 Listening

Listen to the tape on which the directors of Tiltex, a textile company, are discussing Point 5 on this evening's agenda. This concerns the allocation of £60,000 donated by George Smethurst for the goodwill of the company.

Five suggestions have been put forward by the directors of this family company, and on the tape you will hear them discuss these proposals. The proposals are listed below together with the names of the speakers.

As you listen, put a tick in the appropriate column if the speaker is specifically in favour of allocating money to a proposal; put a cross in the appropriate column if the speaker is specifically against allocating money to a proposal.

	Bill	Charles	Mike	Mary	Susan
office accommodation					
workshop					
recreation area					
paintings/antiques					
canteen					

2 Presentation

Here is some of the language you have just heard.
Notice how, during the discussion, the speakers:
i agreed and disagreed *with each other*,
ii agreed and disagreed *with each other's proposals*,
iii expressed *different degrees* of agreement and disagreement.

The expressions below show how these distinctions are made in English.

	with a person	with a proposal
(+ +) Complete agreement	I entirely agree with you. I absolutely agree.	I couldn't agree more. I'm all in favour of that.
(+) Tentative agreement	You are probably right. I'm inclined to agree with you.	I think we can accept that. That is perhaps a good idea.
(−) Tentative disagreement	You could be right, but… Up to a point I'd agree with you, but…	I'm not sure we can accept that. I don't think I'm really in favour of that.
(− −) Complete disagreement	I disagree entirely. I really don't agree at all.	I can't possibly agree to that. That is totally unacceptable.

3 Controlled Practice

In the following exercise use the coded prompts to make appropriate responses to the statements made by A. Where necessary, alternative suggestions have been provided. The first two have been done for you as examples.

1 **A** I think we should spend the money on office accommodation. (+ + with A's proposal)
 B I'm all in favour of that.

2 **A** I think some of the money should be spent on the canteen. (+ with A)
 B I'm inclined to agree with you, but I think some of the money should be spent on antiques.

3 **A** I think we should spend most of the money on the workshop. (+ + with A)
 B _____.

4 **A** I think all of the money should be spent on the recreation area. (− with A's proposal)
 B _____. I suggest that a little of the money should be spent on the canteen.

5 **A** I think we should spend most of the money on office accommodation. (− − with A's proposal)
 B _____. I suggest we spend most of the money on antiques.

6 **A** I think the canteen needs urgent attention. (+ with A)
 B _____. I suggest we pay attention to the recreation area as well.

7 **A** I think the workshop is in a disgusting condition. (+ + with A)
 B _____.

8 **A** I think the best thing we could do at the moment is invest the money in a bank. (+ with A's proposal)
 B _____. I suggest we also invest some of the money in paintings.

9 **A** I think that a new recreation area will solve all our problems. (− with A)
 B _____, I suggest that the working conditions should first be improved.

10 **A** I think we should have more workers on the Board of Management. (− − with A's proposal)
 B _____.

---

4 Transfer

PAIR or GROUP WORK

As the only effective way to practise the language presented in this unit is through discussion, the following discussion topics are suggested. In order to produce sufficient discussion, individuals or groups should take opposing points of view, as in a debate.

1 Having workers on the Board of Management is the only way to solve constant industrial unrest.

2 The responsible manager should always live close to his office.

3 Management is usually to blame for bad industrial relations.

4 A high salary is better than a lower salary and a company car.

5 Tax on cigarettes should be doubled.

Unit 8 Management qualities

1 Listening

In this Unit you will hear an interview with three people who have been called to a panel interview to review their positions within their company.

In the second part of the interview they are asked to give their opinions on what they consider to be the three most important qualities for a good manager.

Before you listen to the tape, look at the table below and mark in the first column the three qualities you consider to be the most important. (Use 1, 2, 3 to indicate the order.) Then listen to the interview and mark on the table the opinions of the three interviewees, John Renolds, Mark Pritchard and Susan Stainton.

	You	John Renolds	Mark Pritchard	Susan Stainton
Communicative skill				
Adaptability				
Creativity				
Sensitivity to others				
Stamina				
Foreign language skill				
Authority				
Leadership				

2 Presentation

Here is some of the language you have just heard.

Notice how it is used:

TO EXPRESS AN OPINION STRONGLY
I definitely think that...
I'm sure that...
I'm convinced that...
I really *do* think that...

TO EXPRESS AN OPINION NEUTRALLY
As I see it, ...
I think...
I consider...
I feel...
In my opinion...

TO EXPRESS AN OPINION WEAKLY
I'm inclined to think that...
I tend to think...

3 Controlled Practice

Each question in this section consists of two sentences which represent a dialogue exchange. The first sentence is A's opinion and the second is B's opinion. In each sentence B disagrees with A. He expresses his disagreement either strongly (S), neutrally (N), or weakly (W).

i Select an appropriate expression from the Presentation section above,
ii use the word or phrase given as a prompt,
iii start each answer with the phrase 'Oh really' to indicate B's disagreement.

The first answer has been done for you as an example.

1 **A** I definitely think that oil supplies will run out before the end of this century.
  B (W) _____ last until then.
  B Oh really! I'm inclined to think they'll last until then.

2 **A** I think our holidays are too short.
  B (S) _____ too long.
  B _____.

3 **A** In my opinion we should increase production of the C414.
  B (W) _____ decrease.
  B _____.

4 **A** I tend to think the most important quality for a good manager is stamina.
  B (N) _____ creativity.
  B _____.

5 **A** I feel we should review the sales figures monthly.
  B (S) _____ fortnightly.
  B _____.

6 **A** I really *do* think we are spending too much on training.
  B (W) _____ not spending enough.
  B _____.

7 **A** I'm inclined to think the Production Department needs reorganising.
  B (W) _____ the Marketing Department.
  B _____.

8 **A** As I see it, the R and D Department should concentrate on developing more products.
  B (N) _____ better.
  B _____.

9 **A** I'm convinced we should accept the terms offered by the employers.
  B (W) _____ reject.
  B _____.

10 **A** I definitely think we should speed up the implementation of Plan A.
   B (N) _____ slow it down.
   B _____.

11 **A** I tend to think we should increase the number of flexitime hours.
   B (S) _____ increase.
   B _____.

4 Transfer

PAIR or GROUP WORK

A Below is the table of qualities which you used in the Listening Section. Now it's your turn to choose the five most important qualities for the manager of tomorrow. Do this individually. When you have numbered your top five, discuss your choice either in pairs or in larger groups, and explain and justify the qualities you have chosen.

Communicative skill	
Adaptability	
Creativity	
Sensitivity to others	
Stamina	
Foreign language skill	
Authority	
Leadership	

B Now note down the five qualities you consider to be most important for the successful company in the 1980's. When you have done this individually, give your opinions to the other members of the group. Discuss the qualities you have chosen.

Unit 9 Pricing policy

1 Listening

On the tape for this Unit is a conversation involving the Sales Manager of a motor agency and two of his salesmen. The problem they are discussing is the sale of the old models which are in their showrooms.

Now listen to the tape. As you listen make a list of the suggestions made by the salesmen in the space below.

1 _____
2 _____
3 _____
4 _____
5 _____
6 _____
7 _____

2 Presentation

Here is some of the language you have just heard.

Notice how it is used to make firm (XXX), neutral (XX) and weak suggestions (X).

FIRM SUGGESTIONS (XXX)
I think we should take a whole-page advert.
Don't you think we should also check around the other agents?

NEUTRAL SUGGESTIONS (XX)
How about reducing the price of the old models by 10%?
Why don't you two prepare the figures?
I suggest that you two work out the costs first.

WEAK SUGGESTIONS (X)
It might be a good idea to keep the price as normal.
What do you think about offering free petrol for 200 miles?

3 Controlled Practice

Use the table to make suggestions for the problems facing your small company. The first one has been done for you.

Problems	Suggested solutions
1 Productivity low	XX Increase automated equipment
2 Lack of worker satisfaction	XXX Diversify job responsibilities
3 Cash-flow shortages	XXX Increase short-term borrowing facilities
4 Long-term investment difficulties	XX Discuss long-term overdraft scheme
5 Increased raw material prices	X Buy in bulk
6 Difficulty in evaluating market potential	XX Improve forecasts
7 Insufficient market coverage	XX Employ more sales reps
8 Poor management-worker relationship	X Increase worker participation in decision-making

1 How about increasing the automated equipment?

2 _____
3 _____
4 _____
5 _____
6 _____
7 _____
8 _____

4 Transfer

GROUP WORK

Discuss and suggest solutions to the following problems:

A *Closed-shop problem*
In a printing firm, one operator does not wish to join the printing union. The other employees refuse to work with him unless he joins. The management are unwilling to put pressure on the operator to join the union.

B *Price-war problem*
An airline company has found itself involved in a price-cutting war. Its competitors are reducing their prices almost daily in order to remain the cheapest on the market.

C *Marketing coverage problem*
A small company has to increase sales to survive. It does not have sufficient sales personnel to compete with its bigger rivals.

Unit 10　Office talk (1)

1 Listening

Listen to the 8 short dialogues in which someone is asking for permission to do something. Was permission granted or refused?

As you listen tick the box which you think gives the answer. Tick Yes if permission was given; tick No if permission was refused.

Dialogue 1　Yes ☐　No ☐
Dialogue 2　Yes ☐　No ☐
Dialogue 3　Yes ☐　No ☐
Dialogue 4　Yes ☐　No ☐
Dialogue 5　Yes ☐　No ☐
Dialogue 6　Yes ☐　No ☐
Dialogue 7　Yes ☐　No ☐
Dialogue 8　Yes ☐　No ☐

2 Presentation

Here is some of the language you have just heard. Notice how it is used to *ask permission*, and to *grant* and *refuse permission*.

Asking Permission	Granting	Refusing	Notes
Do you mind if I leave early?	(No) All right. No. Not at all.	I'm sorry, I can't allow that.	This is a strong refusal. [NB 'Yes' in answer to 'Do you mind'…means a refusal.]
May I smoke?	Yes (of course).	No you may not.	This is a strong refusal.
Can I look at your newspaper?	Well, OK. Go ahead.	I'd rather you didn't.	This is a polite refusal.
negative: Do you mind if I don't join you for lunch?	(No) All right.	Of course you must.	

27

3 Controlled Practice

A Listen to the tape again. Each time you hear someone asking for permission, stop the tape. Practise granting or refusing permission, using the phrases given in the presentation. Then restart the tape and compare your answer with the one on the tape. It does not matter if your answer is not exactly the same. If you find this difficult, use the tapescript to help you.

B Now look at the situations below. Ask permission to do what you want in each case. Write the question in the space provided.

1 It is very stuffy in the room. You want to open a window.

2 You haven't got enough chairs in your office for all your visitors. You want to borrow one from the next office.

3 You are in an important meeting. No-one else is smoking. You want to smoke.

4 Your typewriter is out of order. You want to use your colleague's machine to type your report.

5 You want to talk to your boss about an urgent matter.

6 You have been asked to represent your company at a conference. You don't want to go.

7 You want to see the report your colleague has just written.

8 You find you have left your wallet at home and you have no money. You want to borrow some from a friend to buy your lunch.

9 You have a visitor in your office. You want to make a phone call now.

10 You have been discussing an important matter. You don't want to make a decision immediately. You want to give your answer this afternoon.

4 Transfer

PAIR WORK

Look at the following situations and act them out with your partner.

A

Student A
You think your secretary is very inefficient. You want to dismiss her or to transfer her to somebody else. You discuss the problem with the Personnel Manager. Explain why you are not satisfied with her and ask permission to do something about it.

Student B
You are the Personnel Manager. Listen to the problem. You don't want to dismiss anybody unless there is very good evidence that they are bad workers. You interviewed this girl yourself and you think she should be good. Perhaps your colleague has a personal dislike. Grant or refuse permission as you think best.

This time, change roles.

B

Student B
You have to meet a client to discuss a contract which would be important for your company. However, you don't have a good relationship with him. You think he dislikes you and that it would be better for someone else in the firm to see him. Discuss the problem with your boss and ask permission to pass responsibility on to someone else.

Student A
You are the boss. Listen to the problem. You think he is exaggerating the situation. You don't think there is anyone else in the company who can deal with this client. Grant or refuse permission as you think best.

Unit 11 Wages and prices

1 Listening

Listen to the tape in which the following economic cycle is being discussed:

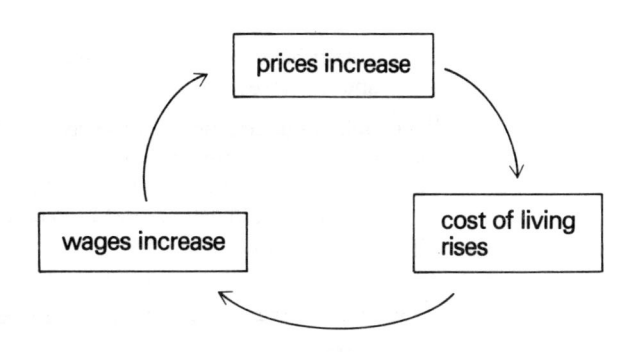

```
          prices increase
         ↗              ↘
  wages increase    cost of living
         ↖              ↙   rises
```

Now listen again and number the stages in the cycle for the two companies below:

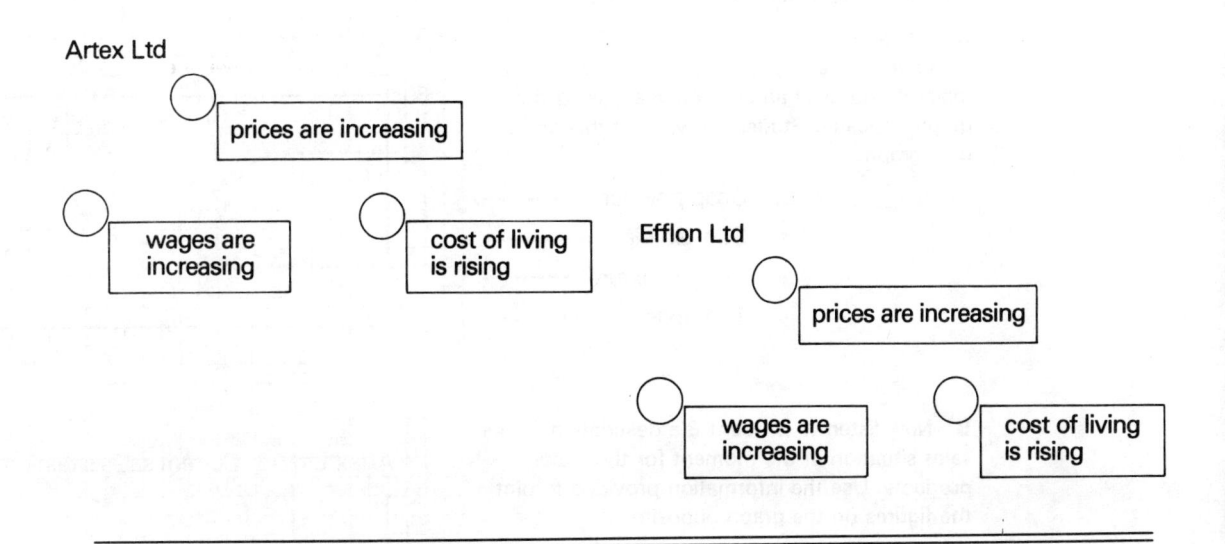

Artex Ltd

○ prices are increasing

○ wages are increasing   ○ cost of living is rising

Efflon Ltd

○ prices are increasing

○ wages are increasing   ○ cost of living is rising

2 Presentation

Here is some of the language you have just heard.

Notice the different uses of the present simple and the present progressive.

PRESENT SIMPLE
It is used to make general statements with no specific reference to time.
Wage demands *open* the cycle.
Employees *ask* for wage increases to match cost of living increases.

PRESENT PROGRESSIVE
It is used to make statements about temporary events with reference to present time.
At the moment Efflon *are negotiating* a pay deal.
At present the employees *are asking* for a 19% increase.

3 Controlled Practice

Complete the following passage with the correct form of the verb in brackets.

As a rule high interest rates _____1_____ (lead to) a credit squeeze, and the present high interest rate _____2_____ (cause) a lot of companies to go bankrupt. Furthermore, at the moment foreign manufacturers _____3_____ (complain) bitterly about our import tariffs.

On the other hand, low interest rates _____4_____ (help) small companies to borrow more easily and low taxes _____5_____ (encourage) private enterprise.

If we look at our situation we can see that for the time being the inflation rate _____6_____ (drop). However, commodity prices _____7_____ (increase) now, but they generally _____8_____ (rise) at this time of year anyway. Although a strong currency usually _____9_____ (mean) export problems, for the time being exports _____10_____ (do) very well. But many small companies _____11_____ (try) to expand too fast and _____12_____ (not analyse) sufficiently the relevant market factors.

4 Transfer

PAIR WORK

Student B
Turn to the Key Section for this unit.

A *Student A*
Describe the sales pattern for Artex Ltd's four major products in an average year, using the graph opposite. Student B will plot this on his own graph.

Soap powder ————
Sun-tan oil – – – – –
Cough mixture – - – - –
Toothpaste ·········

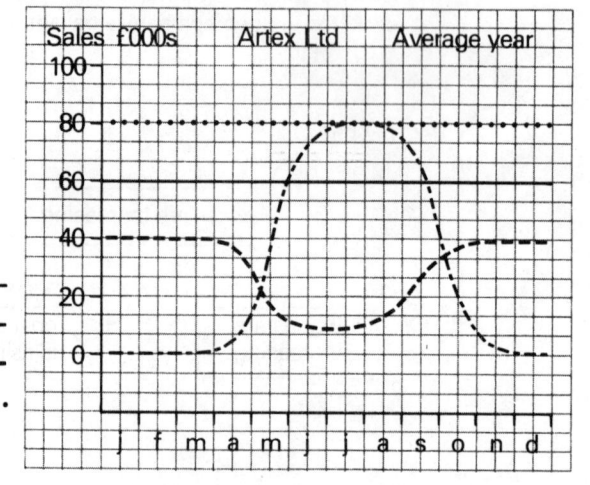

B Now listen to Student B's description of the sales situation at the moment for the major products. Use the information provided to plot the figures on the graph opposite.

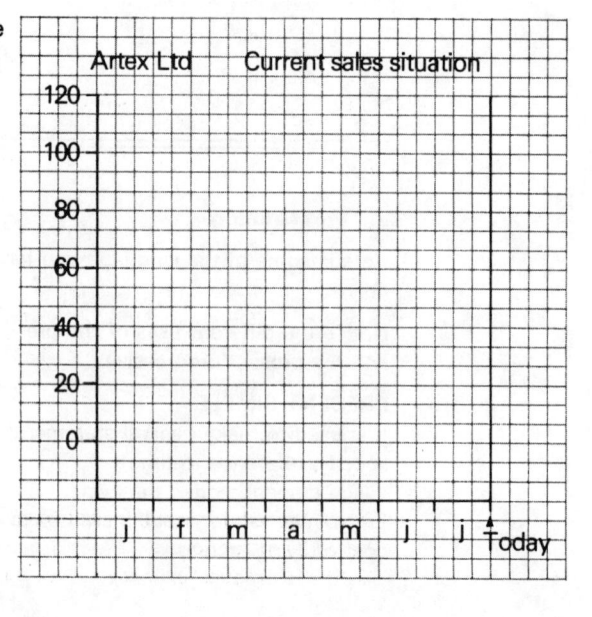

Unit 12

Travel expenses

1 Listening

Listen to the tape on which a salesman is being questioned by a finance manager about a recent business trip. The finance manager is looking for ways of cutting expenses on such trips.

As you listen, number the verbs below in the order they occur. The verbs are arranged alphabetically in their infinitive form (the first two have already been numbered).

to arrive ( )	to finish ( )	to manage ( )
to be ( )	to fly (2)	to read ( )
to catch ( )	to get (1)	to sleep ( )
to come ( )	to go ( )	to spend ( )
to cost ( )	to have ( )	to stay ( )
to eat ( )	to last ( )	to take ( )

2 Presentation

Here is some of the language you have just heard.

Notice how the verbs change when we are talking about events in the past.

REGULAR VERBS
to arrive — I arriv**ed** at 6 o'clock.
to finish — the meeting finish**ed** at 5 o'clock.
to last — the meeting last**ed** 5 hours.

IRREGULAR VERBS
to be — My meeting **was** at 11 o'clock.
to catch — I **caught** the 8 o'clock plane.
to come — I **came** back the next morning.

Remember how we ask questions in the past...
to cost — How much **did** the meal **cost**?
to eat — Where **did** you **eat**?
to stay — **Did** you **stay** in the same hotel?
to take — Which plane **did** you **take**?

NB to be — **Was** it a success?

...and how we make negatives:

I **didn't catch** the evening plane.

Check that you know the past tense forms of all the verbs introduced in this unit before you go on to the practice exercises in the next section.

3 Controlled Practice

A Look at this page from last week's engagement diary.

MONDAY	9 am 1 pm 3 pm	go to board meeting have lunch with boss write up report
TUESDAY	morning: 2 pm	read over report meet son at airport spend afternoon at departmental meeting
WEDNESDAY	3 pm	eat lunch at home catch plane to Paris stay night at agent's flat
THURSDAY	4 pm	visit exhibition in morning fly back to London
FRIDAY	10 am 3 pm	see financial director drive to Manchester

Now complete these sentences:

1 On Monday morning I _____ to the board meeting.

2 After the meeting I _____ lunch with my boss.

3 In the afternoon I _____ up my report.

4 On Tuesday morning I _____ over the monthly sales report.

5 At 2 o'clock I _____ my son at the airport.

6 I _____ the afternoon at a departmental meeting.

7 On Wednesday I _____ lunch at home.

8 At 3 pm I _____ the plane to Paris.

9 I _____ the night at our agent's flat.

10 On Thursday morning I _____ the exhibition.

11 In the afternoon I _____ back to London.

12 At 10 o'clock the next day I _____ the financial director.

13 At 3 pm I _____ to Manchester.

B Now ask for more information about last week's engagements.

Use the prompts below to make your questions.

e.g. How long/board meeting/last?
How long did the board meeting last?

1 where/have/lunch?
2 which report/write up?
3 finish/monthly sales report?
4 plane/arrive on time?
5 when/departmental meeting/finish?
6 what/eat/for lunch?
7 plane/leave/on time?
8 sleep/well?
9 which exhibition/visit?
10 have/a good flight?
11 why/see/the financial director?
12 why/drive/Manchester?

4 Transfer

PAIR WORK

You have received a very bad copy of your boss's report from last week's sales trip and most of the important information is illegible.

Student A
Complete the report by asking Student B to give you the information from the diary entries for the trip in the Key Section.

Student A will have to ask questions like, Where did you fly to on Monday?

Report: Sales trip to S.France, 10-12 March

Monday 10

    10.00   flew to ?.... Good flight, no problems.

    .00   met Mr. Jones - useful contact.

    13.00   had lunch at La ?........ Ideal place for business, good value and relaxed atmosphere.

    16.00   visited ?............

    19.00   went by ?... to Marseilles. Efficient service - arrived in Marseilles at ?.?? prompt.

Tuesday 11

    ?.??   saw main distributor in Marseilles

    12.00   made presentation to ?........

    14.00   went by ?... to Nice where I had dinner with ?... at 19.00.

Wednesday 12

    10.00   appointment at ?........ company where I met M. Leclerc and discussed ?..... arrangements.

    12.00   caught plane to ?..... and arrived ??.??.

Unit 13 Work routines

1 Listening

Listen to the interview in which a Sales Manager describes his job. He talks about each of the duties or activities which he has to carry out, and tells how often he has to do each of these.

As you listen, look at the table below. It lists all the activities which the sales manager has talked about. Try to complete the column on the right. Write down the frequency: how often does he carry out each activity?

	Activities	Frequency
1	work in the office	
2	have meetings with the Finance Manager	
3	report to the General Manager	
4	check the sales figures from all the branches	
5	visit other branches	
6	travel abroad	
7	prepare financial reports	
8	meet customers	
9	deal with important customers	
10	fix targets for the coming year	

Now answer this question:

How often do the company's sales figures fall below target?

2 Presentation

Here is some of the language you have just heard. Notice how it is used to express (A) Definite Frequency and (B) Indefinite Frequency.

A DEFINITE FREQUENCY

once   a day/week/month/year

twice
         an hour

three times

four times

etc.

        every day/every week/every month/every year
           daily   weekly   monthly   yearly,
                                                      or annually

NB   quarterly (usually used for accounts,
       figures, reports etc.)
        = every three months/four times a year

B INDEFINITE FREQUENCY

always
usually
often
quite often
sometimes
occasionally
rarely
never

WORD ORDER

Phrases of definite frequency usually come at the end of a sentence.
I meet the Finance Manager twice a week.

Words expressing indefinite frequency come *before* the verb:
I *sometimes travel* abroad.
I *usually work* in my office.

However, with the verb *to be*, they come *after*:
I *am never* late for meetings.
Sales *are usually* higher in the summer months.

---

3 Controlled Practice

A Look at the graphs below and complete the sentences which describe them. The missing words give the *definite frequency* at which measurements are taken:

1 These are the _____ sales figures for Branch X.

2 These are the _____ figures for the company. These figures are prepared _____ _____ _____.

3 These are the company's _____ results for the past 5 years.

4 The retail audit data are collected _____ _____ _____.

B Look at the table below. How often do you think each group of people buys 'Nutto', a popular chocolate bar with nuts? Complete the table with a number 1 to 5, where 1 = never and 5 = often.

Now write statements about each of the groups. Use one of the words from the Presentation to substitute each number, e.g. if you put 5 by housewives, write: Housewives often buy Nutto.

housewives	
school children	
lorry drivers	
shop assistants	
policemen	
businessmen	
fashion models	

4 Transfer

PAIR WORK

Either *Student A*
Describe your job in terms of the activities you carry out e.g. attend meetings, type letters, answer the telephone etc.

Student B
Ask questions to find out *how often* A does each of these things. Complete the table below and report back to the class. If time, reverse roles and repeat.

Or *Student A*
Imagine yourself in a job e.g. Sales Manager, Bank Manager, Typist and describe the activities you would carry out in that job.

Student B
As Student B opposite.

Activities	Frequency

Unit 14

Company rules and regulations

1 Listening

You are going to hear an extract from an introductory speech given by the Personnel Manager to a group of newly recruited secretaries joining a company. First read the information given below.

Then, as you listen put a tick in the TRUE column if the information you hear corresponds with the information on the sheet, or in the FALSE column if it does not correspond.

The secretaries:	TRUE	FALSE
may choose what time to start work		
needn't work between 10 and 3		
mustn't work less than 37 hours a week		
can claim a maximum of 10 hours overtime per month		
should inform their department heads each Monday of their weekly hours		
must start each day at the same time in any one week		
needn't say in advance what time they intend to finish		
can take 8 days holiday in July		
can take lunch in the canteen		
must buy lunch tickets on Friday for the following week		

2 Presentation

The table below shows the different ideas that the modal verbs *can, could, may, might, must, need* and *should* can express.

may (not)/might (not) can/could	POSSIBILITY
can't, cannot	IMPOSSIBILITY
must (not), mustn't/should (not), shouldn't	NECESSITY/ OBLIGATION
needn't, need not	LACK OF NECESSITY/ LACK OF OBLIGATION
may/can	PERMISSION
may not/can't, cannot	LACK OF PERMISSION
must (not), mustn't/can't, cannot	PROHIBITION
can	ABILITY
can't, cannot	INABILITY

NOTES

1 *may* is more commonly used than *can* to indicate possibility.

2 *should* indicates:
i moral obligation,
You should return things you've borrowed.
ii general obligation, but less forceful than *must*,
I should finish that report this afternoon (but perhaps I won't).
cf. I must finish that report this afternoon (so I definitely will finish it).

3 *can* and *may* are both used to indicate permission. However, *may* tends to be more formal and tentative.
Can I leave this till tomorrow? is more informal and more direct than:
May I leave this till tomorrow?

Now listen to the tape again and notice how these verbs have been used in the Personnel Manager's talk.

3 Controlled Practice

Look at the table below which gives posting information.

The posting information indicates:
latest posting time (for arrival next day in the same town),
suitability (i.e. what can be sent in that category),
where (to post items in that category).

CATEGORY	LATEST POSTING TIME	SUITABILITY	WHERE
1 Postcard	11 a.m.	Routine information	Post-box
2 Letter	4 p.m.	Routine and private information	Post-box
3 Printed paper	9.30 a.m.	Newspapers, journals, and other printed material	Post-box
4 Registered mail	5 p.m.	Valuable written documents	Post-office (not post-box)
5 Package	1 p.m.	Non-bulky goods	Post-office (not post-box)
6 Parcel	12 a.m.	Goods weighing more than 2kg.	Post-office (not post-box)

Examples are given for the sending of postcards. Use the information given to make sentences for the other categories of mail.

1a To arrive next day a postcard must be posted before 11 am.
    mustn't/can't be posted after 11 am.

 b It can/may be used for sending routine information.
    It shouldn't be used for sending private information.

 c It may be posted in a post-box.
    It needn't be posted in a post-office.

Now you continue.

2a _____ before 4 pm.
 b _____ valuable documents.
 c _____ in a post-office.
3a _____ after 9.30 am.
 b _____ newspapers.
 c _____ in a post-office.
4a _____ after 5 pm.
 b _____ valuable written documents.
 c _____ in a post-box.
5a _____ before 1 pm.
 b _____ newspapers.
 c _____ in a post-office.
6a _____ after 12 am.
 b _____ goods weighing more than 2 kg.
 c _____ in a post-box.

4 Transfer

PAIR WORK

(For this exercise try and work together with someone from another organisation.)

Explain and compare your establishments' policies on:
i booking and taking holidays
ii attending seminars/courses in company time
iii retirement
iv examinations.

Unit 15 Plans and strategies

1 Listening

Listen to the extract from a meeting in which the General Manager, the Sales Manager, the Product Manager and the Finance Manager of a small company discuss their plans for the next quarter.

As you listen, complete the flow diagram below. If necessary, listen again.

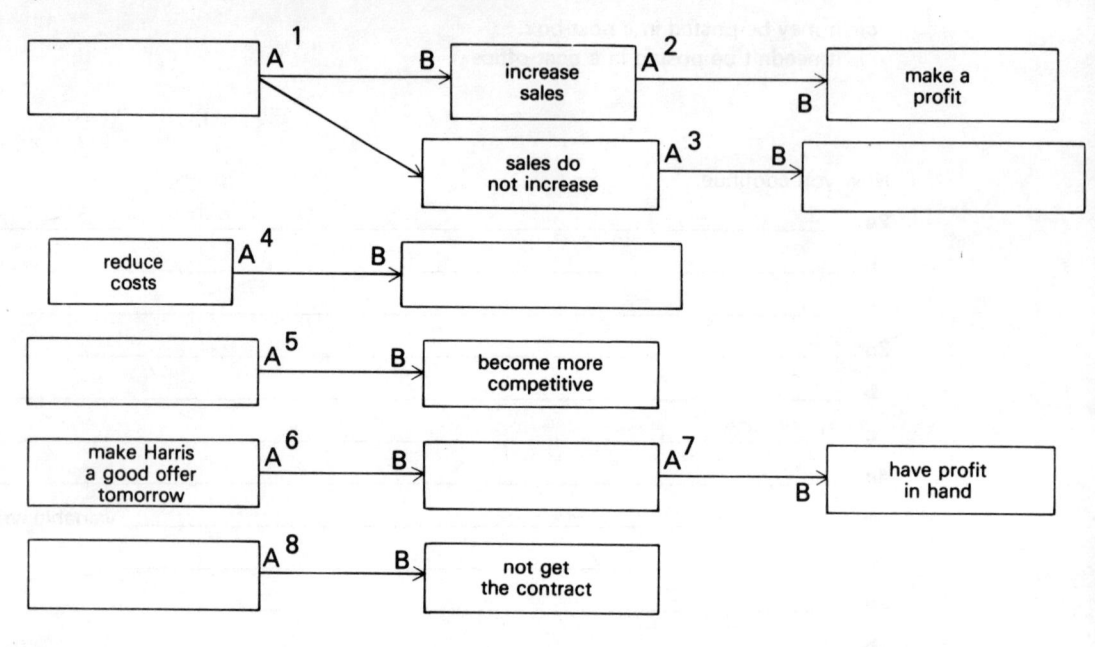

```
[        ] --A1--> B [increase sales] --A2--> B [make a profit]
         \                           
          \--> [sales do not increase] --A3--> B [        ]

[reduce costs] --A4--> B [        ]

[        ] --A5--> B [become more competitive]

[make Harris a good offer tomorrow] --A6--> B [        ] --A7--> B [have profit in hand]

[        ] --A8--> B [not get the contract]
```

2 Presentation

Here is some of the language you have just heard. Notice the difference between the two forms of the conditional.

A condition	result
If we <u>increase</u> sales	we'<u>ll make</u> a profit.
If we <u>go</u> and see Harris	we'<u>ll get</u> the contract.
If we <u>delay</u>	we'<u>ll be</u> too late.
present tense	future tense ('ll = will)
B condition	result
If we <u>reduced</u> our costs	we'<u>d be</u> in a stronger position.
If we <u>increased</u> our spending	we'<u>d be</u> in serious financial difficulties.
past tense	conditional tense ('d = would)

40

In A the speaker sees the condition as a real possibility. He thinks it is quite possible for them to increase sales, go and see Harris or delay too long.

In B the condition is seen as doubtful. The speaker thinks that it is unlikely that they will reduce costs or increase spending.

3 Controlled Practice

A Look again at the flow diagram you completed above. Listen again to the dialogue.

Which of the ideas in the boxes marked with an A were expressed as possible, and which were doubtful?

The numbers below refer to the numbers on the flow diagram. Mark each one: P for possible, D for doubtful. The first one has been done for you.

1 P   5
2   6
3   7
4   8

Now express each A → B using one of the two forms given in the Presentation. Use the appropriate form.

B The Sales Manager of the company is always very optimistic and expresses the conditions below as if they were all real possibilities.

e.g. I make Harris a good offer.
He gives us the contract.
If I make Harris a good offer, he'll give us the contract.

The Finance Manager is a cautious person and expresses the conditions with some doubt.

e.g. We get the contract.
We have difficulties in fulfilling it.
If we got the contract, we'd have difficulties in fulfilling it.

Now do these in the same way.

		condition	result
1	SM	We get the contract.	It gives us money to spend on advertising.
2	FM	We spend the money on advertising.	We lose it.
3	FM	We spend it on capital investment.	It provides strength against inflation.
4	SM	We don't increase our market share now.	We go into a decline.
5	FM	We increase our market share now.	We still need to invest.
6	SM	We beat our competitors now.	Our figures rocket next year.
7	SM	Our figures rocket.	I am able to retire.

4 Transfer

PAIR WORK

You are managers in the company whose situation is described above. You get the important contract from Harris, and now you must decide what to do with the extra income.

Make a list of the possible courses of action. Discuss each one and mark all those you agree on.

Now report back to the class. Treat the points which you agree on as real possibilities. Say why you think they are good ideas.

e.g. We think it's a good idea to spend more on advertising, because if we do that, we'll increase our sales.

The points on which you disagree will be treated as doubtful. Say why you could not agree.

e.g. My colleague says that if we reduced advertising costs we'd save money, but I think we'd lose sales if we did that.

Unit 16

Interview preparations

1 Listening

Listen to the tape on which Paul McIntyre telephones Stuart Wilkinson to sort out some details about four candidates for the post of Production Manager.

Paul has to sit on the interview panel this afternoon. He's got the candidates' names and some background details but the information has got mixed up.

As you listen to their telephone conversation, complete the table below by putting the information in the correct columns. The first one has been done for you.

Name	Previous company	Company product	Product use
John Stevens	Chemico		
Peter Murray			
Harold Harper			
Anthony Short			

Agrico	Biofin	Plastics
Pharmico	Germitex	Fertilizers
Chemico	Pivone	Alcohol
Plastico	Kolopex	Paint

42

2 Presentation

Here is some of the language you have just heard.

John Stevens is the chap *who worked for Chemico*.
Chemico is the company *which makes Pivone*.
Pivone is the product *we put in our alcohol*.

In each sentence the underlined clause gives us additional information; it *defines* the chap/company/product we are talking about.

These defining relative clauses, as they are called, are introduced by

i *who/that* if they refer to a person,

e.g. John Stevens is the chap who/that worked for...

ii *which/that* if they refer to a thing,

e.g. Chemico is the company which/that makes... However, the above relative pronouns may be omitted if they are not the subject of the relative clause,

e.g. Pivone is the product we put in our alcohol. 'We' is the subject, so the relative pronoun is omitted.

Similarly with the sentence below:
e.g. John is the man we've selected for the job.

Now compare the last two examples with the first three.

iii *where* if they refer to a place,

e.g. Manchester is the place where he was born.

or

Manchester is where he was born. (omitting 'the place')

iv *when* if they refer to a time.

e.g. 10.30 is the time when we take our coffee break.

or (more commonly)
10.30 is when we take our coffee break.

---

3 Controlled Practice

Below is a presentation about the new security arrangements at ZYC.

Fill in the gaps with appropriate nouns (where necessary) and relative pronouns. The first one has been done as an example.

'Today I'd like to look at the new security arrangements proposed for ZYC. As you know, ZYC is 1 *the place where* much of our top-secret intelligence research is carried out. And I'd like to introduce Dr Foss. He's 2 _____ has been appointed head of security. Now let's take a look at the proposals. First, the main entrance. That's 3 _____ all employees must pass through to enter the premises. Rather than using conventional identity cards, we are going to issue MC security cards. They are 4 _____ have a series of magnetic lines on them to represent a code number and passname, and they will be checked by a security scanner at the entrance gate. This means that the security box at the entrance will be dispensed with. The security guard, 5 _____ sits there at present, will be moved together with his box to the new security gate. This is 6 _____ will be automatically lowered in the event of an emergency. An emergency is 7 _____ someone attempts to gain entry with an illegal security card. The security gate also activates an alarm system which is simply 8 _____ will ring in the security office and at the same time in the central police station. The security guard on duty is 9 _____ is expected to take immediate action. The security office, 10 _____ the other guards are on alert, is only 30 seconds from the gate and therefore reinforcements can be expected very quickly.'

4 Transfer

PAIR WORK

Student B
Turn to the Key Section for this unit.

A *Student A*
You are an area manager for Trends UK Ltd and are asking Student B to give you information about the subsidiaries in his area. Ask him to define the subsidiaries in terms of
i their products,
ii their managers.

e.g. Tell me about Trends Preston.
    What about the manager? Who's that?

Use the information given to you by Student B to complete the table below.

Subsidiary	Product	Manager Name	Previous post
Trends Swindon	T-shirts	John Philips	manager, Burnley
Trends Rochdale	jeans	Peter Jordan	manager, Swindon
Trends Burnley	shirts	Susan Davis	marketing manager, Swindon
Trends Bradford	anoraks	James Cook	sales manager, Burnley
Trends Preston			
Trends Blackburn			
Trends Doncaster			
Trends Wakefield			

B Student B will now ask you for similar information about the subsidiaries in your area. Define your own subsidiaries in terms of their products and managers.

e.g. Trends Swindon? That's the place where they make T-shirts. The manager is John Phillips. He's the chap who used to be manager in Burnley.

Unit 17   Sales call

1 Listening

Listen to the tape on which a salesman is trying to sell microwave ovens to a company representative of a pharmaceutical company. Now tick the appropriate column for each statement in the box below.

	TRUE	FALSE
The company has a small canteen.		
The company employs 150 staff.		
This includes pharmacists, lab technicians, admin. staff etc.		
They aren't far from Axton.		
It isn't a very long way to go home for lunch.		
All the staff eat in the canteen.		
The company representative often eats in the canteen.		
He doesn't enjoy eating in the canteen.		
He would eat in the canteen if there was a bigger choice.		
The rest of the staff would definitely eat in the canteen if there was a greater choice.		

2 Presentation

Here is some of the language you have just heard.

Notice the different ways of asking questions.

DIRECT QUESTIONS

How many staff do you have?
Do you eat in there yourself?
Why is that?

As these questions tend to be more abrupt, they are not always appropriate for polite enquiries.

INDIRECT QUESTIONS

Could I start by asking you if you have a canteen here for your staff?
I wonder if I could take a few minutes of your time to tell you about our product?
Could you tell me what interest your microwave ovens are to us?

These questions, which are all asked at the beginning of the sales call, usually sound more polite.

(See also Unit 2.)

STATEMENT QUESTIONS

These questions either use tags as in
It's a long way for your staff, isn't it?
So you don't really enjoy eating there, do you?
or
So, most of them eat in the canteen, is that right?
or use rising intonation to mark the statement as a question:
The same would be true of your staff?

They are often used to check information which the questioner has inferred and to encourage the answerer to make an appropriate reply. They are particularly useful, therefore, in a sales call.

3 Controlled Practice

You are meeting a representative of a company called Petrometers Ltd. They are hoping for a distribution arrangement in the Middle East. Your boss, who is away on business, has left a list of information he needs about the company. Use the list below and the language presented above to ask appropriate questions. Remember, a statement question is often useful when checking information and an indirect question is often used for polite inquiries to start with.

Find out:

1 full company name

2 British owned company?

3 number of employees

Check:

4 the main factory is situated near London

5 chief company product is oil drilling meters?

Find out:

6 who they sell to in the UK

7 which Middle East country is their main export market

8 if there are any other important export markets

Check:

9 no other distributors?

Find out:

10 suitable date for a visit to the factory.

4 Transfer

PAIR WORK

Student A

Take the part of a personnel manager and interview Student B for the post of computer programmer at Petrometers.

In the first section below is some information about the candidate which the personnel office already has. In the other is the additional information you need to find out. Start by checking the information given using statement questions. The candidate can also ask questions about the company, the salary, holidays or any other information he feels he needs.

Student B

Turn to the Key Section for this unit.

Information about the candidate

Name: C. Baines
Age: 24
Address: 54 New Street,
　　　　　Birmingham B4
Education: Quinton Grammar School,
　　　　　　Birmingham
　　　　　　University of Manchester:
　　　　　　degree in mathematics
Experience: 2 years with the Savings Bank as trainee computer programmer.

Information to find out

First name?
Date of birth?
Married or single?
Any children?
When did he leave?
How many years?
1st, 2nd or 3rd class degree?

Knowledge of Cobol?
Knowledge of other computer languages?
Reason for leaving previous post?
Ambitions?

Unit 18

Office Talk (2)

1 Listening

Listen to the conversation between a manager and one of his senior salesmen. As you listen, tick the appropriate column for each statement below.

	TRUE	FALSE
John has finished the report.		
He hasn't done the sales figures yet.		
John hasn't had much work.		
John has already moved house.		
He and his wife need a smaller place.		
The children want more space.		
A copy of his report has gone to the Board.		
The Board is going to decide whether to accept his report.		

2 Presentation

Here is some of the language you have just heard. Notice how the present perfect is used.

A *Present perfect with yet and already*

Yet is used in questions and negative statements.
Have you finished the report yet?
We haven't moved house yet.

Already is used in positive statements.
They've already decided to accept whatever recommendations you make.

B *Present perfect with since and for*

Since is used to indicate a point of time.
We've been in our present house since 1977.

For is used to indicate a period of time and is often used with the progressive form of this tense.
We've been looking for a bigger place for the last 6 months.

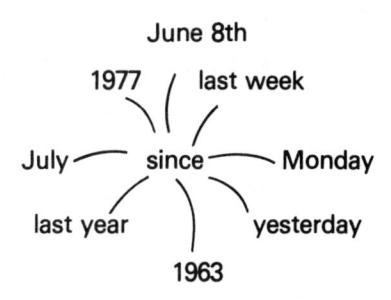

```
           June 8th
      1977    last week
        \  |  /
July  —  since  —  Monday
        /  |  \
   last year    yesterday
           1963
```

```
    a week      two years
        \      /
6 months  — for —  an hour
        /      \
  a long time   a couple of days
```

3 Controlled Practice

The following table shows in note form the development and achievements of a small chemical company over the last few years.

If the note is followed by YES/NO, make a YET/ALREADY sentence. If the note is followed by point/period of time, make a SINCE/FOR sentence.

The first two have been done for you as examples.

1	WE /BREAK INTO/ THE AMERICAN MARKET	NO
2	WE / PRODUCE CHEMICAL FERTILIZERS	1975
3	THE COMPANY / EMPLOY AN AMERICAN AGENT	YES
4	AMERICAN DEALERS / SHOW INTEREST IN OUR PRODUCTS	LAST 2 YEARS
5	WE / SIGN CONTRACTS WITH AMERICAN DEALERS	NO
6	OUR M.D./ VISIT NEW YORK	YES
7	THE MARKETING DEPT. / CARRY OUT RESEARCH	1979
8	THE R & D DEPT. / WORK ON A SPECIAL PRODUCT RANGE	6 MONTHS
9	THEY / COME UP WITH 2 NEW PRODUCTS	YES
10	WE / STUDY AMERICAN REGULATIONS	NO
11	WE / EXPORT SPECIAL PRODUCTS TO OTHER COUNTRIES	1978
12	THE SALES DEPT. / TRAIN REPS FOR THE AMERICAN MARKET	YES

1 We haven't broken into the American market yet.

2 We have produced chemical fertilizers since 1975.

3 _____

4 _____

5 _____

6 _____

7 _____

8 _____

9 _____

10 _____

11 _____

12 _____

4 Transfer

PAIR WORK

Student A
Complete the tables below by finding out whether actual figures correspond with planned figures for the various targets in the sales and production departments.

Student B
Use the completed table in the Key Section to respond to student A's questions.

Example Student A Have you increased the number of sales reps by two?

Student B No, not yet.

Student A How many have you employed?

Student B So far, only one.

Sales Department

Items	Year 1 Plan	Actual
No. of new sales reps	+ 2	
Sales target	£250,000	
New customers per sales rep.	+ 5	
Sales costs	- 10%	
Sales training (weeks)	20	
Appointment of agents	+ 6	

Production Department

Items	Year 1 Plan	Actual
No. of employees	- 5	
Production target (units)	+ 2,000	
New plant (machines)	+ 3	
Production costs	- 10%	
Training (weeks)	10	

Unit 19 Office talk (3)

1 Listening

Listen to the tape. Mr Brown, who has just got back to the office after a two week holiday, wants to know what's been happening during his absence. You will hear him talking to his Personal Assistant.

As you listen, put a tick in the TRUE column if the information you hear corresponds with the information on the sheet, or in the FALSE column if it does not correspond.

	TRUE	FALSE
Mr Brown had good weather on his holiday.		
Nothing important has happened in the office.		
There have been a number of changes in the Marketing Department.		
Taylor has taken over Fairburn's job.		
Three new marketing posts have been created in the Marketing Department.		
Johnson decided to leave the company.		
Mr Brown went to Barcelona for an intensive language course last year.		
The Saudi company rejected the terms offered by Mr Brown's company.		

2 Presentation

Here is some of the language you have just heard.

Notice the main difference between the use of the past tense and the use of the present perfect tense.

A The past tense refers to a point of time or a period of time in the past.
I arrived here yesterday.
I spent three years in Amsterdam. While I was there I worked in our head office.

B The present perfect tense refers to a period of time (either stated or understood from context) connected to the present.

What's happened? (Inferred period of time: between the time I was last in the office and now.)

Three important things have happened. (Inferred period of time: during the last two weeks.)

I've been waiting for that course since last year. (Stated period of time: since last year.)

3 Controlled Practice

The following sentences may need correction. Read the whole paragraph first. Then make corrections where they are necessary.

1 Last year we have made our first contract with Rotaronga.

2 We were very surprised when they accepted our terms.

3 And therefore we had an agent on the ground since then.

4 Six months ago we delivered the first instalment of the goods.

5 Immediately, they have been very pleased with the quality of the products.

6 Since that time we waited for a second contract.

7 So, our Marketing Manager has visited them a few weeks ago to discuss future business.

8 When he came back, he was very enthusiastic.

9 Despite political problems in Rotaronga, our policy was always to do business wherever and whenever possible.

10 And we believe that this policy has, up to now, always paid off.

4 Transfer

PAIR WORK

Student A
You have just returned from holiday and want to find out what has happened to various colleagues (WHO column in your table). Start by asking your partner what has happened to each colleague (WHAT column). Then ask when it happened (WHEN column) and finally why it happened (WHY column).

Student B
Respond to your partner's questions, using the completed table in the Key Section.

WHO	WHAT	WHEN	WHY
Max			
Sheila			
Peter			
Fred			
Julie			
Clare			

Unit 20 Past appointments, future engagements

1 Listening

Before listening to the tape, look at the list of events below.

1 Carter's talk with Pearson
2 ITA meeting
3 Taylor leaves for Paris
4 Sales figures to be ready
5 Taylor to look at the figures
6 Trade Fair
7 Marketing Director returns from the USA
8 Board meeting
9 Meeting with Marketing Director
10 Carter's accident
11 Carter's appointment with the doctor.

Now listen to the conversation on the tape, in which you will hear when each of these events took place, or will take place. As you listen, write the number of each event in the correct space on the time-plan underneath.

last month	last week	this week			TODAY				week-end		next week					
		Sat	Sun	Mon	Tue	Wed	Thu	Fri	Sat	Sun	M	T	W	T	F	morning
																afternoon
																evening

2 Presentation

Here is some of the language you have just heard. Notice how it is used to refer to *point of time* and *time relating to now*.

A POINT OF TIME

These expressions refer to a specific time, and they remain unchanged no matter what the time or the day is now.

Notice the use of prepositions:
AT + time on the clock
at 10 o'clock, at five past ten etc.
AT + special time
at Christmas, at Easter

ON + day or date
on Monday, on 12th June etc.

IN + month, season or year
in January, in the winter, in 1979

FROM a time TO a time
I worked in London from 1970 to 1978

BETWEEN a time AND a time
Phone me between 2 and 4 this afternoon.

BY indicates a deadline or latest time
We must finish this by 4 o'clock.

B TIME RELATING TO NOW

These expressions depend on the time and the day which is now.

Look at these time scales:

i TODAY

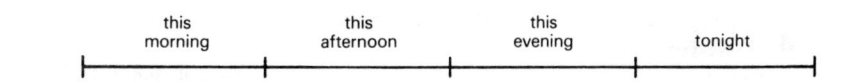

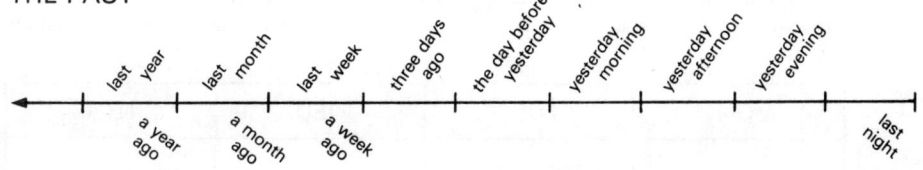

this morning | this afternoon | this evening | tonight

ii THE PAST

last year / a year ago — last month / a month ago — last week / a week ago — three days ago — the day before yesterday — yesterday morning — yesterday afternoon — yesterday evening — last night

iii THE FUTURE

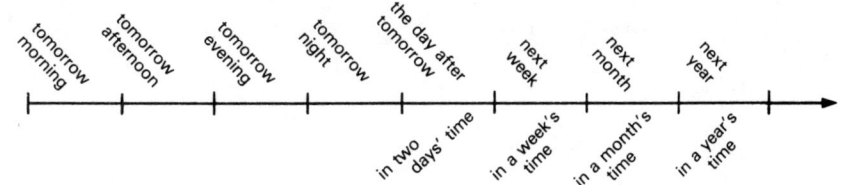

tomorrow morning — tomorrow afternoon — tomorrow evening — tomorrow night — the day after tomorrow / in two days' time — next week / in a week's time — next month / in a month's time — next year / in a year's time

iv HOURS

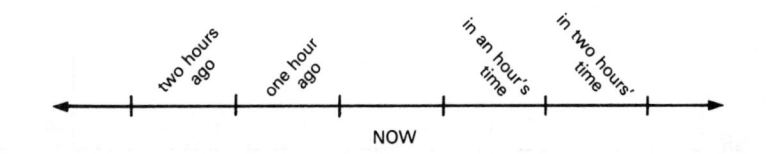

two hours ago — one hour ago — NOW — in an hour's time — in two hours' time

3 Controlled Practice

A Expand the following telegrams which your boss has received:

e.g. ARRIVING 6.45 AM SUNDAY. HERR SCHMIDT
   Herr Schmidt is arriving at quarter to seven on Sunday morning.

1 SEE YOU THURSDAY 16.30 REGARDS JOHN

2 MISS PEABODY TRAVELLING USA 31ST MAY RETURNING JULY

3 PLEASE PHONE FRIDAY 9–10 AM. THANKS FRANK MARTIN

4 CANT MAKE TONIGHT. SUGGEST FRIDAY 8 PM OR WEEKEND. PLEASE PHONE ASAP. REGARDS DAVID SIMON.

B Today is 14th March. It is 11.30 am. Express each of the following in relation to the time now.

e.g. Mr Smith is coming on 15th March.
   He is coming tomorrow.

1 Mr Ferguson is retiring on 24th March.

2 I'm meeting Jane for lunch on March 14th at 12.30.

3 Mr Smith phoned on 14th March at 10.30 am.

4 The last meeting was held on 1st March.

5 Your letter arrived on 12th March.

6 I returned from Rome on 7th March.

7 The report must be ready by 15th March in the afternoon.

8 We are having dinner together on 14th March in the evening.

4 Transfer

PAIR WORK

Decide which of each pair will be the Boss and which the Secretary.
It is Monday and the Boss wants to know his timetable for this week.

He will ask questions like: 'What am I doing this afternoon/tomorrow morning?'
The Secretary will reply according to the timetable in the Key Section.
The Boss should enter his engagements into his own, blank timetable below.

MON.	TUE.	WED.	THU.	FRI.

Unit 21

Making arrangements

1 Listening

Listen to the tape on which you will hear a telephone conversation between a training manager and an engineer. The training manager wants to find out when the engineer will be available to attend a one-week language course.

As you listen, indicate, in the right-hand column, the week numbers for the various engagements listed in the left-hand column.

The first one has been done for you.

ENGAGEMENTS	WEEK NOS.
Finish design plans for Kuwait plant	
Prepare 6-monthly report	
Aid study-group visit	
Trade fair in Switzerland	
Visit Kuwait subsidiary	36
Holiday in Miami	
Visit distributors in Midlands	
Monthly meeting with Maintenance Dept.	

When you have completed the table, decide which of the weeks would be most suitable for the engineer to attend the course.

2 Presentation

Here is some of the language you have just heard.

Notice how it can be used to indicate different degrees of certainty about future actions.

CERTAIN ACTIONS
i Fixed timetable
For activities in the future which are fixed by a timetable, we can use the present simple.

e.g. Our flight leaves Miami on Friday.
   The train gets in at 9.30 tomorrow morning.

ii Fixed arrangements
For activities in the future which are fixed by arrangement, we generally use the present progressive.

I'm flying out to Kuwait on the Monday.
He's going to the Midlands to visit our distributors.
We're spending a fortnight in Miami.

INTENDED ACTIONS
For activities in the future which are intended, we use:
i going to ......
ii intend to ......
iii plan to ......
iv aim to ......

I'm going to work on my six-monthly report.
A study group is going to visit us.
I intend to finish the design plans for the Kuwait plant.
When do you plan to be back?
I aim to help out with the German study group.

NEUTRALLY EXPRESSED ACTIONS
We use: will ......

The six-monthly report will take me most of the week.
The study group will be here for three days.

3 Controlled Practice

Expand the notes in the left-hand column to express the degree of certainty indicated in the right-hand column. The first one has been done for you.

A	1	Plane/depart/6.30 Monday	fixed timetable
	2	I/visit/HQ in Brussels	fixed arrangement
	3	I/see/the Marketing Manager	intended action
B	1	Where/you/spend your holidays?	intended action
	2	We/take the train to Marseilles.	fixed arrangement
	3	What on earth/you/do/there?	intended action
	4	We/not/stay/there.	fixed arrangement
C	1	When/you/have/report ready?	intended action
	2	It/be/ready/this afternoon.	neutral action

A 1 The plane departs at 6.30 on Monday.
    2 _____
    3 _____

B 1 _____
    2 _____
    3 _____
    4 _____

C 1 _____
    2 _____

---

4 Transfer

PAIR WORK

A Discuss with your partner your holiday plans. Note down the certainty of your partner's plans.

B Discuss with your partner your work plans e.g. future career, examinations, further education, training etc. Note down the certainty of these plans.

Unit 22 Recruitment procedures

1 Listening

Listen to the dialogue in which the stages in a company's recruitment procedure are discussed.

As you listen, number the stages below in the order they occur (the first two stages have already been numbered).

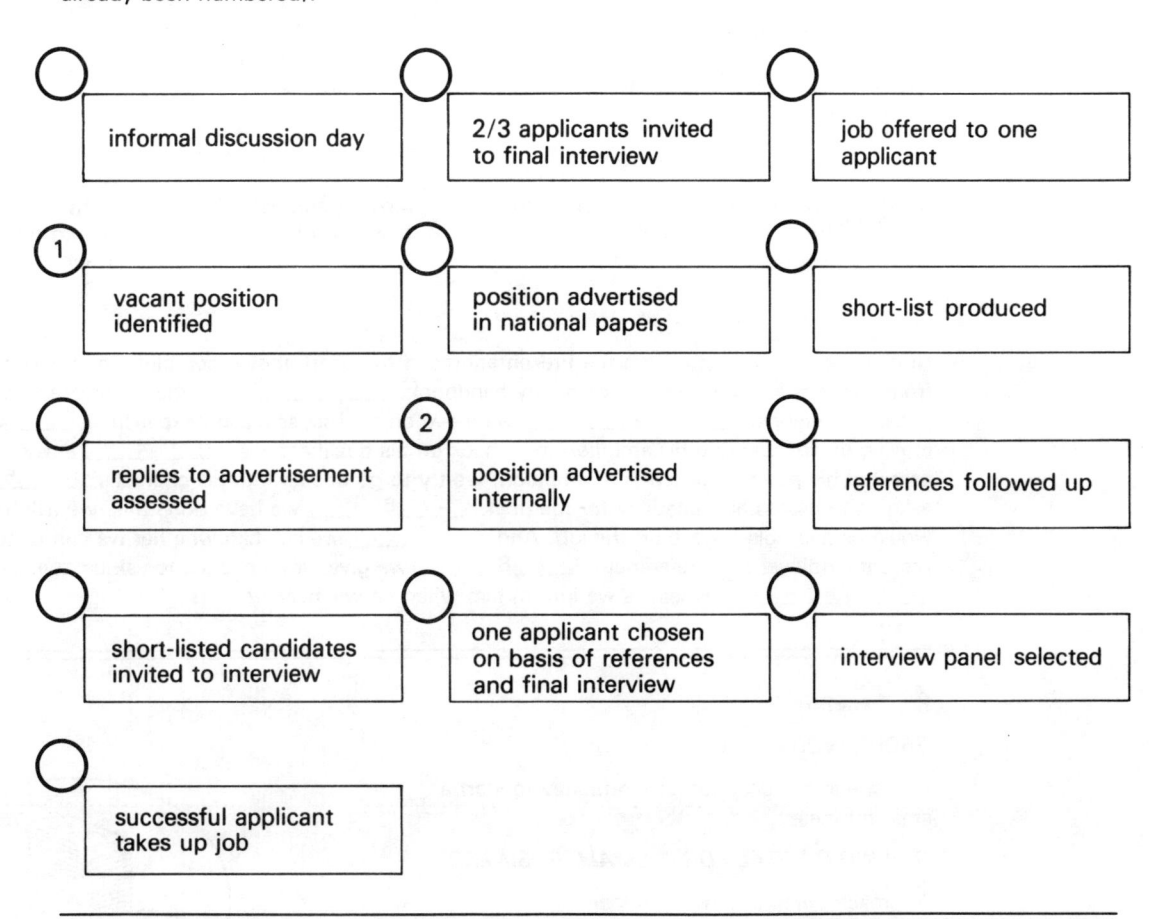

- ( ) informal discussion day
- ( ) 2/3 applicants invited to final interview
- ( ) job offered to one applicant
- (1) vacant position identified
- ( ) position advertised in national papers
- ( ) short-list produced
- ( ) replies to advertisement assessed
- (2) position advertised internally
- ( ) references followed up
- ( ) short-listed candidates invited to interview
- ( ) one applicant chosen on basis of references and final interview
- ( ) interview panel selected
- ( ) successful applicant takes up job

2 Presentation

Here is some of the language you have just heard.

Notice how it is used to indicate the beginning of a process, the different stages in a process and the end of a process.

BEGINNING OF A PROCESS
First(ly)...
Initially...
In the first place...
To start with...

STAGES IN A PROCESS
(and) then...
the next step/stage is...
Once X has been done, Y is done
As soon as..., ...
Prior to/Before...
In the meantime...

END OF A PROCESS
Finally, ...
Lastly, ...
The last step/stage is...

3 Controlled Practice

Look at the flow chart below showing the sequence of questions/areas covered in interviewing a candidate.

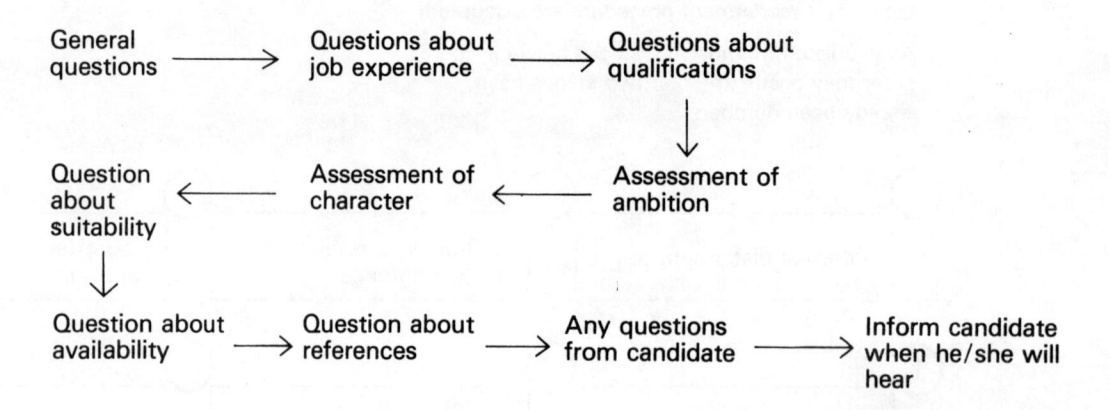

General questions → Questions about job experience → Questions about qualifications ↓
Question about suitability ← Assessment of character ← Assessment of ambition
↓
Question about availability → Question about references → Any questions from candidate → Inform candidate when he/she will hear

Now, using the language from the Presentation and the chart above, complete the following passage from *Interviewing Guidelines*, a company handbook: ____1____, the candidate is asked a few general questions. ____2____, we move on to discuss his job experience. ____3____ moving on to assessing his ambition, we check on his qualifications. ____4____ we have assessed his potential in terms of ambition, we try to go deeper into his character. ____5____, we ask him to assess his suitability for the post. ____6____ we have done this, we ask him when he would be available to take up the job. And ____7____ we ask him whether we can contact his present employer for a reference. ____8____, we give him a chance to ask us questions and ____9____ he leaves we inform him when he will hear from us.

---

4 Transfer

GROUP WORK

Here are some ideas for raising money to start a small business.

RAISING CAPITAL FOR A SMALL BUSINESS

Approach bank for long-term loan.
Approach friends for low-interest long-term loan.
Find a 'backer' and offer partnership in return for finance.
Mortgage your house to raise money.
Approach bank for short-term overdraft.
Gamble a small bank overdraft at a casino.

First arrange them in the order you think best.
Add any other ideas you have to the sequence.

Then one member of the group should present the sequence he thinks best to the group and compare it with other members' ideas. Try to agree on the best sequence.

Unit 23 Deciding company policy

1 Listening

Listen to the tape on which John, Peter and Mike, the directors of a company manufacturing bathroom tiles, are discussing the future of the company. Each of them has slightly different views on the best way to survive in the market place.

In the table below:
✓ = *must* follow plan y (i.e. it's necessary)
− = *needn't* follow plan y (i.e. it's not necessary)
× = *mustn't* follow plan y (i.e. it's necessary not to)

Now listen to their discussion and as you listen put the initial of the speaker in the appropriate column in the table below. The order of the speakers is John (J), then Peter (P), and then Mike (M).

The first answer has been done for you.

	✓	−	×
concentrate only on the home market			
concentrate only on the foreign market			
concentrate on both the home and foreign markets	J		
borrow money from the bank			
grow very quickly			
increase product range			

2 Presentation

Here is some of the language you have just heard.

Notice some of the ways of expressing the categories of NECESSITY/OBLIGATION.

✓	−	×
must have to have got to need to	needn't don't need to haven't got to don't have to	mustn't

The following rules for use of the above verbs are given as a rough guide:

1 Written regulations and orders
– *must/mustn't*
The report must be completed by tomorrow morning.
The budget mustn't be exceeded.

2 Internal obligation – *must/mustn't*
I must finish the report before I go home. (It's my personal responsibility)
I mustn't leave the report till next week.

3 External obligation – *have to/don't have to*
I have to finish the report before I go home. (the boss said so)
I don't have to write a complete report.

4 Informal – *have got to/haven't got to*
I'm sorry, but we've got to leave now. (either internal or external obligation)
We haven't got to be back till next week.

59

3 Controlled Practice

Company A and Company B have different strategic plans for next year. Use the table below to make sentences, firstly about Company A, and secondly about Company B. The first sentence has been done for you.

e.g. We must (have to/have got to/need to) increase production. Now you continue with Company A, and then Company B.

PLAN	COMPANY A	COMPANY B
Increase production	✓	—
Take on more staff	✗	✓ (Production Dept.)
Develop new products	—	✓ (Research Dept.)
Invest in new machinery	✓ (French subsidiary)	—
Increase prices to retailers	✓	✗
Spend more on advertising	—	✗ (Promotion Dept.)

4 Transfer

PAIR or GROUP WORK

Discuss some of the things
  we've got to do
  we don't need to do } in order to try and solve
  we mustn't do
the following world problems:

1 Inflation
2 Unemployment
3 The imbalance of wealth
4 East-West tension

Unit 24

Product description

1 Listening

Listen to the tape on which you will hear a presentation introducing a new model and comparing it with its predecessor. As you listen fill in the information in the table below.

	B1368	B1500
Length		
Width		
Height		
Weight		
Performance (units per minute)		
Service intervals		

2 Presentation

Now look at some of the language used to talk about dimensions, measurements and specifications.

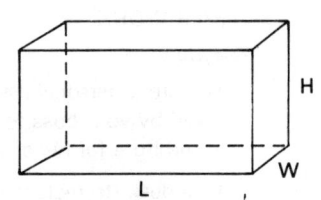

LENGTH
How long is it? It's 50 cm long.

WIDTH
How wide is it? It's 30 cm wide.

HEIGHT
How high is it? It's 20 cm high.

WEIGHT
How heavy is it? It weighs 50 kg.
How much does it weigh?

How big is it? is a general question about measurements.

L = length
W = width
H = height
L × W = area
L × W × H = volume

AREA/VOLUME
What's its area?   Its area is...   or It has an area of...
          volume?   volume is...   a volume of...

MEASUREMENTS, DIMENSIONS, SPECIFICATIONS
What are its measurements?   Its measurements
          dimensions?   dimensions   are...
          specifications?   specifications

CAPACITY
How much can it hold?   It can hold...kg.
          does it carry?   It carries...kg.

Now listen to the tape again and see how some of this language has been used.

3 Controlled Practice

Using the diagram of a container lorry, write down appropriate questions and answers.

Max Load: 20 tons
Capacity: 80 fridges

Length	Q	_____?
	A	_____
Width	Q	_____?
	A	_____
Height	Q	_____?
	A	_____
Base Area	Q	_____?
	A	_____
Volume	Q	_____?
	A	_____
Load (max. weight)	Q	_____?
	A	_____
Holding Capacity (Fridges)	Q	_____?
	A	_____

---

4 Transfer

PAIR WORK

Student A

You are a personal assistant. You have been asked by your boss to order the following items of furniture for his office:

1 a desk (to replace his existing desk, which has become too small)

2 a book-case (to hold 150 catalogues)

3 an open-hanging filing system (to accommodate 200 separate items)

Find out from the supplier (Student B) the range of models available for each item of furniture. Then decide which model for each of the three items best fits into the plan below of your boss's office.

Student B
Look at the Key Section for this unit.

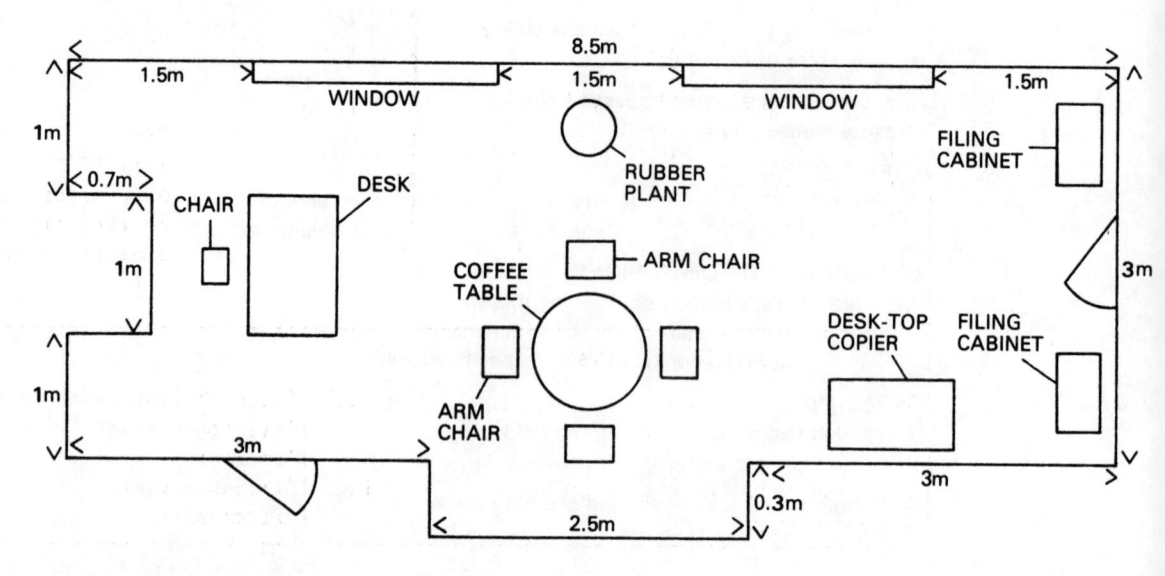

Unit 25

Value, price and efficiency

1 Listening

Before listening to the tape, look at the information given in the table about four types of heating systems. The cost of installation and running costs are not given in the table.

Listen to the dialogue in which Mr James asks advice about which system would be best for his offices. As you listen, fill in the information about cost of installation and running costs in the spaces in the table.

	electric panel radiators	hot air vents	gas-fired radiators	electric ceiling heating
Can you adjust the temperature easily?	YES	NO	YES	?
Is it clean?	YES	NO	YES	YES
Installation cost				
Running cost				

2 Presentation

Here is some of the language you have just heard.

Notice how you can ask and answer questions on price and value.

Questions about price		Replies
How much is...? are...? How much does X cost? How much does it cost to install? How much do you pay for...? What's the price of...? What's the cost of...? What do you pay for...?	X is are costs The price is You pay	£250 about £5 between 15p and 20p 20p per pound/a pound per/a litre/square metre etc.
Questions about value		
Is X cheap? expensive? Is X cheap to run/install etc.?	(Yes).	It's very cheap/expensive/dear. It's very good value. It's a bargain.
	(No).	It's not good value. It's poor quality.

3 Controlled Practice

Ask and answer questions on each of the following. Ask about the cost/price of the item; then give the cost or price as stated on the right.

e.g. How much does it cost to fly from London to New York?
(It costs) About £340.

1	to fly from London to New York (normal excursion fare)	£340
2	a Sunday newspaper in Britain	15 – 28p
3	a London theatre ticket	about £5
4	a telephone call from UK to France	30p/minute
5	an apartment in London	£100/week or more
6	apples (in Britain)	20p/pound
7	petrol (in Britain)	£1.80/gallon
8	a cup of coffee	25p
9	steak	£2/pound
10	to travel by train from London to Edinburgh	about £30
11	records	about £5 each
12	land (outside the city centres)	about £3,000/acre

4 Transfer

PAIR WORK

Student A
You have been allocated £3,000 as a settlement allowance for your new posting to Dariland, Africa.

This is to be spent on furnishings for a flat and suitable clothes.

Ask your partner for the prices of the various items listed below and decide how to spend the money.

Student B
Use the listed prices in the Key Section to answer student A's questions.

Student A copy

Furnishings for flat
Settee
Armchairs
Double bed
Single beds
Wardrobe
Chest of drawers
Fridge
Fridge freezer
Freezer
Dining table
Dining chairs

Clothes
Lightweight suits
Cotton shirts
Cotton trousers
Lightweight jacket (blazer)
Shoes

Unit 26

Inflation

1 Listening

Listen to the tape on which you will hear an excerpt from a business presentation. The financial director describes the development of the rate of inflation.

As you listen, complete the graph.

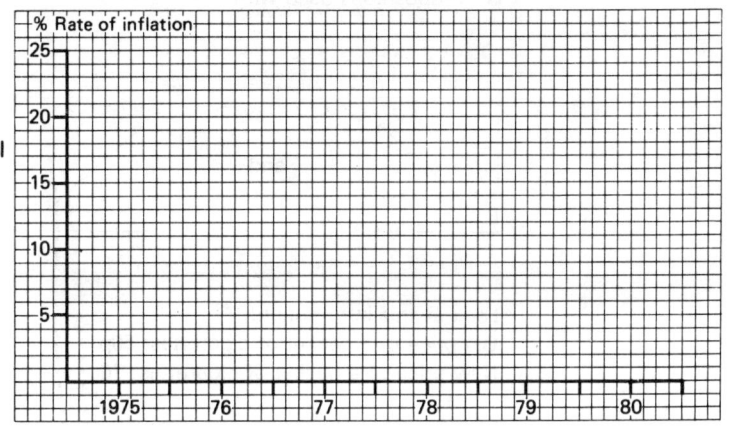

2 Presentation

Below you will find some of the language you have just heard:

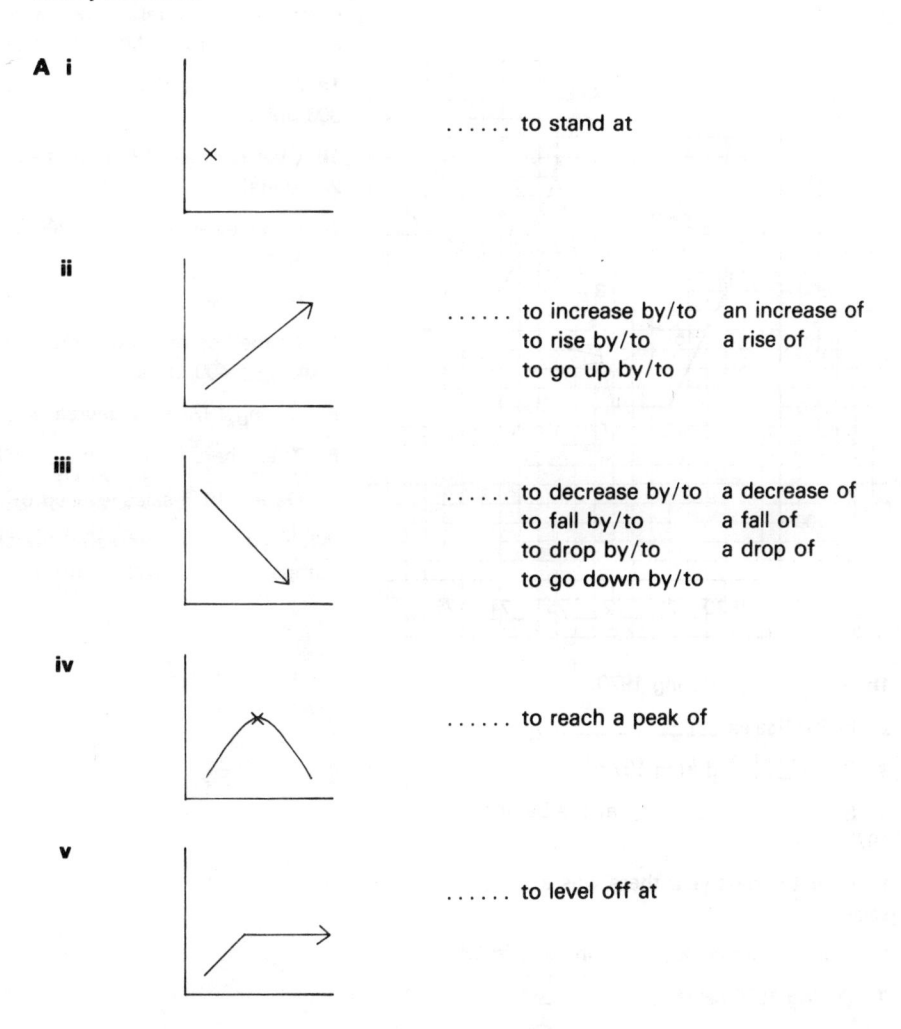

A

i ...... to stand at

ii ...... to increase by/to   an increase of
    to rise by/to   a rise of
    to go up by/to

iii ...... to decrease by/to   a decrease of
    to fall by/to   a fall of
    to drop by/to   a drop of
    to go down by/to

iv ...... to reach a peak of

v   ...... to level off at

65

B Prepositions used with

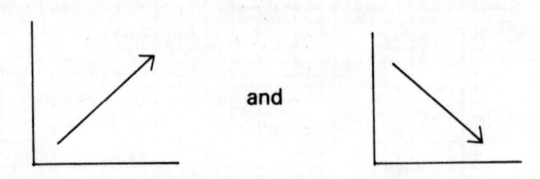

and

Look at this information:
Old price of a packet of cigarettes: 60p
New price of a packet of cigarettes: 70p

We can express this change in price in two ways using a verb
i Cigarette prices increased *by* 10p.
ii Cigarette prices increased *to* 70p.

We can express this change in price in one way using a noun
i There was a price increase (or rise) *of* 10p.

Similarly we say
i Fresh fruit prices fell *by* 5% last week.
ii The price of apples dropped *to* 20p a pound.
and
i There was a fall in price *of* 5%.
or **ii** There was a price decrease *of* 5%.

---

3 Controlled Practice

A Look at the graph and complete the sentences below by writing one word in each blank.

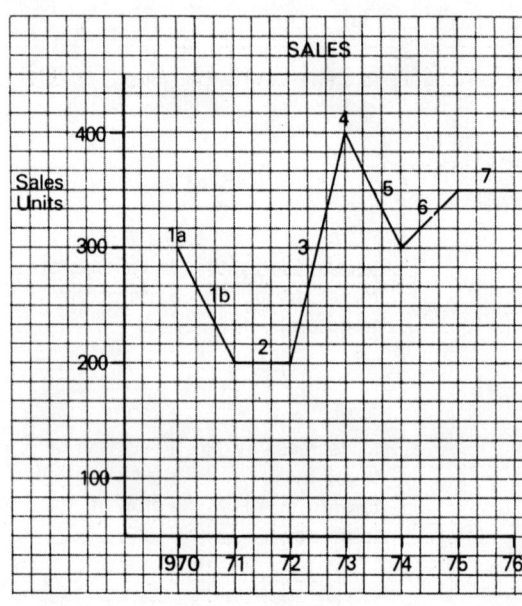

1b Sales _____ during 1970.

2 In 1971 sales _____ _____.

3 Sales _____ during 1972.

4 Sales _____ __ _____ at the beginning of 1973.

5 Over the next year there was a _____ in sales.

6 Then there was a _____ in sales in 1974.

7 During 1975 sales _____ _____.

B Now look again at the same graph (which also shows sales units on the vertical axis) and complete the sentences below with an appropriate preposition – *to, at, of* or *by*.

1a At the beginning of 1970 sales stood ____ 300 units.

1b Over the next 12 months sales dropped ____ 200 units.

2 Sales levelled off ____ 200 units for 12 months.

3 Sales rose ____ 200 units during 1972.

4 At the beginning of 1973 they reached a peak ____ 400 units.

5 During 1973 they decreased ____ 300 units.

6 Then there was a rise ____ 50 units in 1974.

7 During 1975 sales levelled off ____ 350 units.

When you have completed the sentences, compare your answers with the key copy.

4 Transfer

PAIR WORK

Student B
Turn to the Key Section for this unit.

A *Student A*
Look at the completed graph of ice-cream sales below. Describe the ice-cream sales to Student B who will complete the graph in the Key Section.

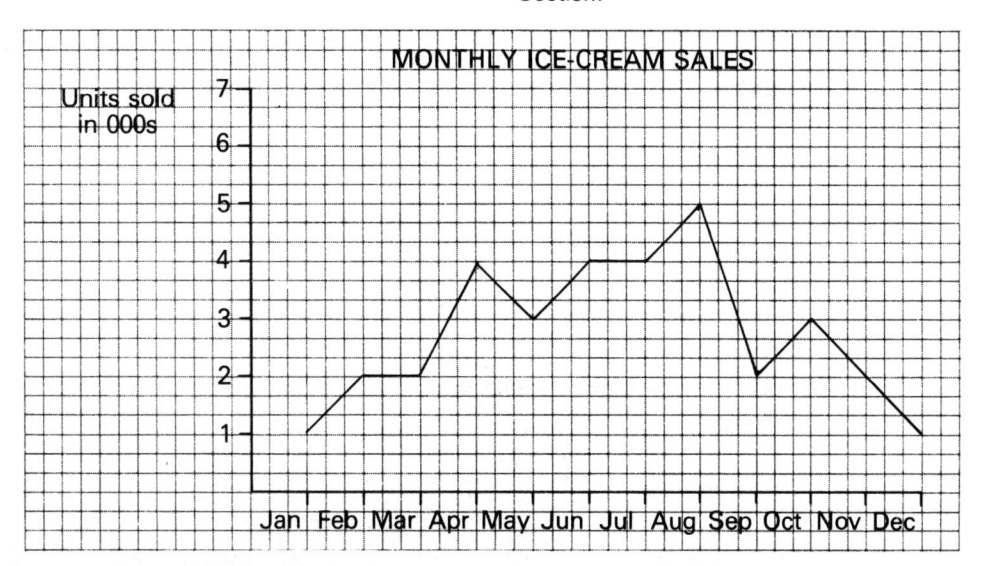

MONTHLY ICE-CREAM SALES
(Units sold in 000s; Jan–Dec)

B Now Student B will describe the traffic density figures to you from his graph in the Key Section. Listen carefully and complete the graph below.

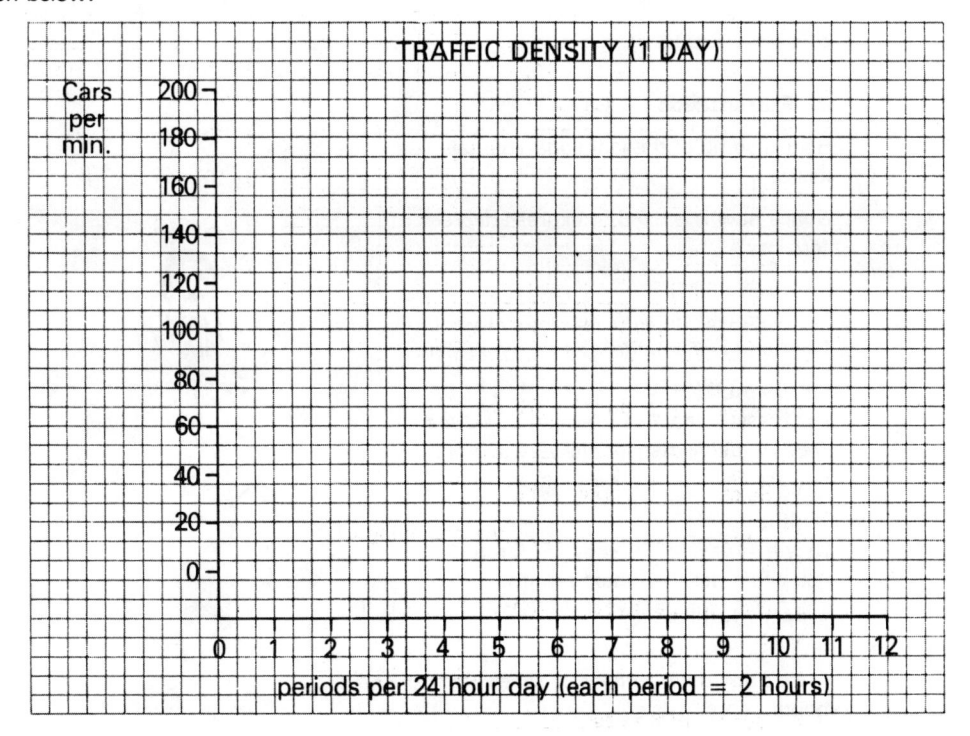

TRAFFIC DENSITY (1 DAY)
Cars per min. (0–200) vs periods per 24 hour day (each period = 2 hours), 0–12

Unit 27 Delivery dates

1 Listening

Listen to the tape on which a clothes retailer is talking to his suppliers about the delivery dates of various items of clothing. As you listen, indicate on the table below whether the delivery months are certain, probable, possible or improbable.

Use the following symbols:
** = certain
* = probable
? = possible
X = improbable

	February (next month)	March	April	May	June
Men's suits					
Sports jackets					
Dresses					
Ladies' sweaters					
Swimsuits					
Skirts					

2 Presentation

Here is some of the language you have just heard.

Notice how it is used to express degrees of certainty.

CERTAINTY(**)
The suits *will certainly* be ready in March.
The skirts *will definitely* be ready in March.

PROBABILITY (*)
The dresses *should* be delivered in June.
We'll *probably* manage delivery in April.
You *are likely to* receive them in June.

POSSIBILITY (?)
They *may/might* be ready in March.
You *could* get them next month.

IMPROBABILITY (X)
I'm afraid that's *unlikely*.
There's not much chance of receiving them next month.

3 Controlled Practice

Use the table to complete the sentences below.
The first one has been done for you.

PRODUCTION TARGETS

	1000	2000	3000	4000	5000
Jan	*	X			
Feb	**	?	X		
Mar	**	*	X		
Apr	**	**	?		
May	**	**	*	?	
Jun	**	**	**	X	

               is likely to
               will probably

1 In January, production <u>should</u> reach 1000 units.

2 However, it _____ reach 2000 units in January.

3 In February, we _____ produce 2000 units.

4 In March, there's _____ reaching 3000 units.

5 In April, the company _____ produce 2000 units

6 and we _____ reach 3000 units.

7 In May, the company _____ produce 3000 units,

8 and we _____ go as high as 4000.

9 In June, production _____ rise to 3000 units,

10 but there's _____ reaching 4000 units.

4 Transfer

PAIR WORK

Student A
You are in charge of your company's vehicle purchasing department. Place an order with your partner for the following vehicles. Also find out when they can be delivered.

6 Ford Taunus 1600 saloons
4 Ford Granada 2000 saloons
4 Ford Fiesta 1100 saloons
10 Ford Escort estate cars
10 Ford Transit vans

Student B
You are responsible for taking fleet car orders for Ford. Note down your partner's requirement for vehicles and use the information in the Key Section to respond to his questions about delivery dates.

Unit 28 Sales

1 Listening

Listen to the tape. A Sales Manager of a Sports Equipment company gives a presentation about the differences between forecast and actual sales.

As you listen, complete the table with the appropriate figures.

Products	Forecast sales	Actual sales
Tennis equipment	£450,000	
Squash and badminton		£180,000
Golf equipment	£100,000	
Winter sports	£250,000	
Football	£110,000	
Hang-gliding		£25,000

2 Presentation

Here is some of the language you have just heard.

Notice how it is used to express *similarity* and *difference*.

SIMILARITY

Forecast sales *were exactly (the same) as* actual sales.

Forecast sales *were almost/nearly the same as* actual sales.

In the hang-gliding section, *as* in the tennis section, sales were on target.

Sales of footballs, *like* sales of golf equipment, did not reach their target.

DIFFERENCE

Forecast sales *differed from* / *were different from* } actual sales.

There was a big *variance* / *difference* } between forecast and actual sales.

Sales of tennis rackets, *unlike* sales of table tennis bats, reached their target.

3 Controlled Practice

Use the information in the completed table and the language presented above to complete the following sentences.

1 Actual sales of tennis equipment _____ forecast.

2 Actual squash and badminton sales _____ forecast.

3 In the golf equipment sector, _____ in the winter sports sector, there _____ between actual and forecast sales.

4 Football sales, _____ those of squash and badminton equipment, _____ the forecast.

5 Sales of hang-gliding equipment, _____ golf equipment, _____ forecast.

6 _____ forecast, sales of tennis equipment reached £450,000.

7 Golf equipment sales, _____ winter sports sales, did not reach their target.

4 Transfer

PAIR WORK

Student B
Turn to the Key Section for this unit.

Student A
Present the information in Table A which shows the % income tax paid on income earned in Molravia.

Student B will now present information telling you the % tax paid on income earned in Caucasia. Use the information to complete Table B below.

TABLE A

Income in US $	% tax
0-2,000	0
2,000-3,000	20
3,000-5,000	30
5,000-10,000	50
10,000-20,000	70

TABLE B

Income in US $	% tax
0-3,000	
3,000-5,000	
5,000-7,000	
7,000-10,000	
10,000-15,000	
15,000-20,000	

Students A and B
Now point out the similarities and differences between the tax systems in the two countries.

Finally work out how much tax individuals would pay if they were earning the following incomes. Student A should calculate for an individual living in Molravia and Student B for an individual living in Caucasia.

Incomes 1 $2,500
         2 $3,500
         3 $6,000
         4 $9,000
         5 $15,500

Now discuss the similarities and differences.
e.g. In Molravia, as in Caucasia, a person earning $1,000 pays no tax.

Unit 29 Market share developments

1 Listening

Listen to the tape on which the regional marketing managers for West Germany, France and the UK answer questions about the growth of market share. Their boss, the marketing manager for Europe, first describes development in Europe. As you listen, complete the table below.

	W. Germany	France	UK	Europe
1977	18%		15%	
1978		22%		19%
1979			23%	

2 Presentation

Here is some of the language you have just heard. Notice how it is used to compare and contrast.

COMPARISON
Our market share in France in 1979 is *better than* in Europe as a whole. (Basic comparison.)

Our market share in France in 1978 is *even better than* in Germany. (This suggests that our share in Germany is already very good.)

Our market share in Germany in 1979 is only *two points higher than* in 1977. (This indicates a specific difference in market share.)

The basic comparison (better, higher, lower, etc.) can be modified to indicate the degree of difference. The modifying words can be grouped together as follows:

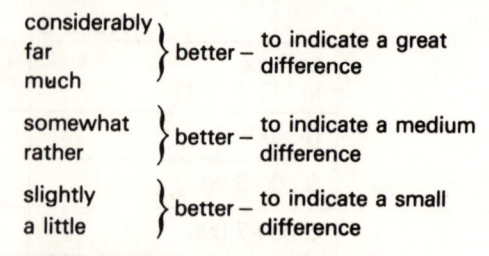

considerably ⎫
far   ⎬ better – to indicate a great difference
much   ⎭

somewhat ⎫
         ⎬ better – to indicate a medium difference
rather   ⎭

slightly ⎫
         ⎬ better – to indicate a small difference
a little ⎭

CONTRAST
Our market share in West Germany increased slowly. *However*, we still made a profit.

Although we made a profit, our market share was low.

3 Controlled Practice

Use the information in the table and the language above to complete the following sentences. Where appropriate indicate a specific difference and a degree of difference. For the purposes of this exercise consider that

```
0 – 2 points   = a small difference
3 – 6 points   = a medium difference
above 6 points = a great difference
```

The first one has been done for you.

1 In 1977, market share in W. Germany was *4 points / rather higher than* in France. *However*, in 1979, market share in France was *8 points / considerably higher than* in W. Germany.

2 _____ UK market share in 1978 was only 18%, in 1979 it was 3 points _____ in W. Germany.

3 French market share in 1977 was only 12% _____, in 1979 it was _____ the figure for Europe as a whole.

4 _____ UK market share was _____ the figure for Europe in 1978, it was the same in 1977 and 1979.

5 Market share in W. Germany reached 21% in 1978. _____, in 1979 it was only _____.

6 _____ market share in Europe increased by 8% from 77 to 79, in W. Germany it only increased by _____.

7 Between 1977 and 1978, UK market share increased more _____ French market share.

4 Transfer

PAIR WORK

Student B
Turn to the Key Section for this unit.

Student A
Describe the development of market share in the car industry in Caucasia by comparing and contrasting home-produced car sales with foreign-produced car sales. Student B will use the information to draw up a graph.

MARKET SHARE —
Domestic v. Foreign Cars   Caucasia

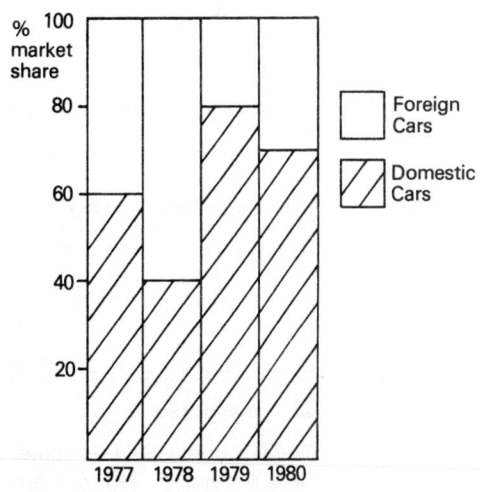

Now listen to Student B's description of market share in Molravia and use it to complete the graph below.

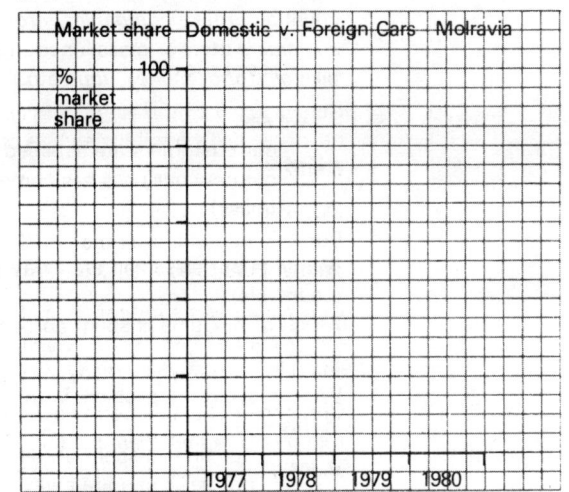

Market share Domestic v. Foreign Cars   Molravia

Now discuss market share development in the car industry in the two countries. Use as much of the language you have learned in this unit as you can to compare and contrast the developments.

73

Unit 30 End of year report

1 Listening

Listen to the tape on which you will hear an extract from an end of year presentation given by the General Manager of Inventa Ltd, a firm which produces office equipment.

As you listen put a tick in the TRUE column if the information you hear corresponds with the statement below, or in the FALSE column if the information does not correspond.

	TRUE	FALSE
A few of the sales staff did not attend the meeting.		
All of the company's products have had a successful year.		
None of the company's products have fallen below the sales target.		
A few of the company's customers have asked for an increased product range.		
Most of the company's customers are satisfied.		
All the questionnaires have now been processed.		
Most of the ideas put forward were unreasonable.		
The company intends to implement a few of the suggestions.		

2 Presentation

The table opposite lists some of the items you have just heard used to express *amount*, ranging from *all of* to *none of*. Notice that in some cases the expression of amount phrase depends on the type of noun it accompanies, count(able) (like *companies, products, customers* etc.) or mass/uncountable (like *oil, food, money, time* etc.)

So we say

All of our customers are satisfied. (countable)
our new business has come from the Gulf. (mass)

but

Many of our salesmen are away on business. (countable)

Much of our time is spent abroad on business. (mass)

We can avoid the problem with *much* and *many* in this way:

A lot of our time is spent abroad.
our salesmen are away on business.

but we cannot simplify the amount words in these examples:

We are going to implement **a few of** your suggestions. (countable)

I want to take **a little of** your time. (mass)

	any noun	count nouns	mass nouns
■■■■	all (of)		
■■■□	most of		
■■□□	a lot of	many of	much of
■□□□	some of		
▪□□□		a few of	a little of
□□□□	none of		

NB The amount words introduced in this unit deal with the situation where we are talking about all, part of or none of a specific or definite total.

Compare the following:
The company invested **some of** its money. (part of a definite amount)
The company invested **some** money. (an indefinite amount)

74

3 Controlled Practice

Look at the letter below. Each sentence has an amount word missing. Rewrite the sentences and include an appropriate amount word or phrase.

```
            CHEMICO FERTILIZERS LTD

R J Stewart
27 Scotts Lane
Athelstaneford
Hants.          FJW/hy      18 August 1982

Dear Bob,

Here's   1    our latest news. You know for
tactical reasons I can't tell you   2    it.

This year we're going to send   3   our salesmen
on a training course. This is because   4   our
sales personnel did not reach their targets last
year, and   5   our customers said they were not
100% satisfied with our service.

We're sure that   6   our staff can improve their
sales techniques. Of course we can't send   7
them at the same time, but we hope that   8   them
can take part in the course before the end of next
year. The company has also decided to send   9
its top managers to America for a short intensive
training course. So you can see we're investing
   10   our money in training.

We've spent   11   time discussing labour
relations in   12   our recent meetings, and
fortunately   13   the strikes we feared has
happened yet. I think   14   the British common
sense is returning.

     15   us wish you a happy retirement.

              Frank.
```

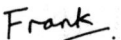

4 Transfer

PAIR WORK

Transonics Ltd is a company manufacturing electronic components. For the last three years they have been trying to break into the European market, but without much success. Over the last 18 months home sales, which were previously good, have been decreasing, and as a result company morale is at a low point. Student A (from the Marketing Department) and Student B (from the Personnel Department) are discussing informally how *they* would allocate this year's training budget.

Student A

You believe that the company's problems could be solved by making the sales personnel more effective and put forward the following priorities for allocation of the budget:
intensive English courses for the company's top salesmen,
intensive courses in the latest marketing strategies for all sales personnel,
visit to America for selected marketing personnel.

Student B

You believe that low morale is at the root of the company's problems, and put forward the following priorities for the allocation of the budget:
extra-mural courses in a wide range of subjects for all personnel,
courses in labour relations for selected personnel from all departments,
courses in effective communications for selected personnel.

In each pair, try and reach a compromise agreement on the allocation of the training budget, saying how much of the money you will give to each scheme. Use as much of the language presented in this unit as you can.

Key Section

Units 1–30

This section contains:
i tapescripts and keys to the Listening exercises
ii answers to the Controlled Practice exercises
iii information for the Transfer section where required.

Unit 1 Greeting friends and strangers

1 Listening

TAPESCRIPT

- **A** 'I'd like to introduce you to Mr Dale. He's from Oregon.'
- **B** 'Pleased to meet you, Mr Dale. My name's King, George King.'
- **A** 'Let me introduce you two. Mr Smith, this is Mr Lyle.'
- **A** 'John, this is Peter.'
- **B** 'Nice to meet you. What line are you in?'
- **A** 'How do you do. I'm Henry Dixon.'
- **B** 'How do you do. My name's Kent, Charles Kent.'
- **A** 'Hello, my name's Susan.'
- **B** 'Nice to meet you. Mine's James.'
- **A** 'Good morning, Mr Black. How are you?'
- **B** 'Very well, thank you, Mr Howard. I hope you are well too.'
- **A** 'Hello, Jane. How are you?'
- **B** 'Oh, I'm fine. What about you, Phil?'

MATCHED NAMES

F	Mr Black	—	Mr Howard
F	Mr Smith	—	Mr Lyle
F	Mr Dale	—	George King
I	John	—	Peter
F	Henry Dixon	—	Charles Kent
I	Susan	—	James
I	Jane	—	Phil

3 Controlled Practice

1 '*I'd like* to introduce you to Mr Kline.'
'Pleased to meet you, *my name's* Harvey, Joseph Harvey.'

2 'Mary, *this is* Mark.'
'Nice to meet you.'

3 '*How do you do*. I'm Graham Stanton...'
'*How do you do.* My name's Clark,...'

4 '*Hello*, my name's Chris.'
'Hello, *mine's* Sarah.'

5 'Hello, Max. *How are you?*'
'I'm fine. *And you?/What about you?*'

6 '*Good afternoon,* Mr Ross. How are you?'
'Very well thank you. *I hope you are well too,*
　　　　　　　　　Mr Stanton.'
　　　　　　　　　How are you, Mr Stanton?'

7 'Let me *introduce you two*. Mr Carne, *this is* Mr Saxon, a colleague of mine.'

Unit 2 Requesting travel information

1 Listening

TAPESCRIPT

TRAVELLER Could you tell me please the time of the first morning plane to Frankfurt?

GIRL Yes. The first plane leaves at 8.15.

TRAVELLER Thanks. And can you tell me when it arrives so that I can let my secretary know?

GIRL It arrives at 10.00 but it may be a little late because the weather forecast is bad.

TRAVELLER I see. Do you happen to know the time of the last plane this evening then?

GIRL Well, there's one at 11.15 but it's fully booked I'm afraid.

TRAVELLER Oh. Well, I wonder if you'd let me know at my hotel if there's a cancellation on that flight. I'd be very grateful.

GIRL Yes, of course I'll do that for you. What's your number?

TRAVELLER 3596. Thank you. Now could you tell me how I can get to Leicester Square please?

INFORMATION REQUESTED

1 time of first morning plane to Frankfurt.
2 the time of arrival.
3 time of last plane this evening.
4 phone hotel.
5 hotel phone number.
6 way to Leicester Square.

3 Controlled Practice

The first parts of the requests are interchangeable.

1 Could you tell me what time the first plane leaves for Paris?

2 Do you happen to know if the hotels are cheaper in Birmingham than in London?

3 I wonder if you'd tell me what the best way to travel from London to York is?

4 I wonder if you'd let me know if there is a seat available on the 2.30 flight?

5 Can you tell me how much a first class ticket to Edinburgh costs?

6 Do you happen to know if the airline company recently increased its prices?

7 Could you tell me if I have to change at Manchester?

8 I wonder if you'd tell me which airport the plane leaves from?

9 Do you happen to know why there are no flights on Sunday?

10 Could you tell me if the flight is going to be delayed because of the fog?

4 Transfer

Student B
Use the information below to answer Student A's questions.

Models	Basic hire	Mileage charge	Insurance	Minimum hire time
Mini	£7 a day	first 200 miles free; then 2p per mile	£2 per day	24 hours
VW Golf	£10 a day	first 150 miles free; then 3p per mile	£5 per day	24 hours
Peugeot 504	£12.50 a day	first 120 miles free; then 4p per mile	£8 per day	48 hours

Unit 3   Arranging accommodation

1 Listening

TAPESCRIPT

A Good morning. Midland Hotel.
B Good morning. This is Jane Stevens from Daxia. I'm trying to arrange accommodation for a number of visiting businessmen from abroad, and I'd like to know a little about the facilities that your hotel has to offer.
A Well, the Midland is a 3-star hotel and we are situated five minutes from the centre of town.
B Uh-huh. And are you on the main road?
A No, we are on a side street, and all the rooms are very quiet.
B And what about a restaurant?
A Well, we find that most of our clients prefer to eat out, and as there are plenty of restaurants in the vicinity, we have only a small restaurant – but we do serve hot food in the evening.
B I see.
A Of course we do have a bar – the Cellar Bar – which has a very intimate atmosphere.
B And what about entertainment at the hotel? Do you put on any dances?
A No, I'm afraid we don't.
B And just a couple of final questions. Do you have either a swimming pool or a sauna?
A No, not in the hotel, but there's a pool with a sauna just round the corner.
B Well, thanks very much for the information. Bye.
A Bye.

A Kings Hotel.
B Good afternoon. My name is Jane Stevens from Daxia. I'm just arranging accommodation for a number of foreign businessmen who are coming here next month. I wonder if you could tell me what facilities your hotel has to offer.
A Yes, certainly. Well, as you probably know, we are not in town. In fact it's eight miles from the hotel to town. The hotel is set in its own grounds and the surrounding countryside is very beautiful and very peaceful. So your guests would certainly be assured of a quiet and restful stay.
B And how about a restaurant?
A Yes, we have a large restaurant which caters both for residents and non-residents. It tends to be quite full around this time of year, but residents, of course, get priority.
B Uh-huh.
A We also have two bars – one of which is exclusively for residents.
B How about evening entertainment? Any dances?
A No, I'm afraid we don't hold them any more. We used to, but now people prefer to go into town for a night out.
B I see. And what about a swimming pool or a sauna?
A Yes, we've recently had a sauna installed and it is extremely popular with our guests.
B And a swimming pool?
A No, not yet, unfortunately.
B Well, thanks very much for the information. Bye.
A Bye.

A Morning. Central Hotel.
B Good morning. This is Jane Stevens from Daxia. I'd like to find out a little about the facilities offered by your hotel.
A One moment, please. I'll just put you onto booking enquiries.

C Booking enquiries.
B Good morning. My name is Jane Stevens from Daxia. Could you tell me a little about the facilities offered by your hotel?
C Yes, certainly. The Central is right in the middle of town, next to the railway station, and is very convenient for people arriving or leaving by train.
B Does that mean that the hotel is quite noisy?
C Well, I wouldn't say that we are exactly a country hotel. Yes, I suppose it is quite noisy.
B How about restaurant facilities?
C No, I'm afraid we haven't got a restaurant here. Of course there are plenty in the vicinity. All we have is a snack-bar which serves light refreshments.
B Do you have a bar?
C Yes, we do.
B And what about evening entertainment?
C Well, we have a dance in the bar every Saturday evening. And that's open to both residents and non-residents.
B Uh-huh, good. Anything else in the way of facilities?
C Yes, we also have a sauna – that's only for residents. And next year we shall have our own swimming pool.
B Well, thanks for the information. Bye.

COMPLETED TABLE

	Hotel 1	Hotel 2	Hotel 3
Name of hotel	Midland Hotel	Kings Hotel	Central Hotel
Location	5 minutes from centre of town	8 miles from town	In the middle of town
Noisy/quiet	Quiet	Quiet	Noisy
Restaurant	Small	Yes	No. Snack bar
Bar	Yes	Yes	Yes
Dancing	No	No	Yes
Sauna	No	Yes	Yes
Swimming pool	No	No	No

Hotel allocation
Jean Mason
– Kings Hotel.
Enrico Marietti and Claude Leclerc
– either the Midland Hotel or the Central Hotel.

3 Controlled Practice

A Smiths Components.
B Good morning. This is Paul Peters of Spracken Spares. Could I speak to Mr Bramhall in the Dispatch Section?
A I'm sorry. Who did you want to speak to?
B Mr Bramhall in the Dispatch Section.
A One moment, please.
  I'm afraid he's on the phone at the moment. Could you hold on a minute or would you rather leave a message?
B No, I'll hang on.
C Dispatch Section.
B Hello. Is that Mr Bramhall?
C Yes, speaking.
B Good morning. This is Paul Peters from Spracken Spares.
C Good morning, Mr Peters. What can I do for you?
B I'm phoning to find out about the delivery of the X428's we ordered last week.
C Well, I've just this minute dispatched them to you and they should arrive this afternoon.
B Good. That's what I hoped you'd say. Thank you. Bye.
C Bye.

4 Transfer

A Asking for information

Student B Answer the phone as bank receptionist.

Connect caller.

Answer the phone as foreign section clerk and give requested details of exchange rates from the table opposite.

B Complaining

Student B Answer phone as travel clerk at Supertours.

When Student A starts explaining his/her problem, tell him/her that it would be better to talk to the manager. Connect him/her with manager.

As manager explain that Student A is first person to complain about the Lagunda holiday.

Explain that Lagunda is a holiday resort renowned for its night-life; it could hardly be quiet.

Explain that in the brochure it was explicitly stated that mostly local food would be served.

Explain that you are not in a position to refund any money; if Student A wishes, a complaint could be made to the tour operator which organised the holiday.

	Buying	Selling
	(Molravian dollars)	
Austria	162·3	163·8
Belgium	60·8	61·9
Canada	11·8	12·2
Denmark	46·2	48·0
France	47·6	48·4
Finland	40·3	41·5
Germany	20·7	21·3
Holland	38·9	39·9
US	12·2	12·7
UK	5·0	5·2

Unit 4 Checking information

1 Listening

TAPESCRIPT

A Dialogue 1

RECEPTIONIST	Good morning. May I help you?
MR LIDDLE	Yes. I'd like to speak to Mr. Watt, please.
RECEPTIONIST	What's your name, please?
MR LIDDLE	Liddle. Terry Liddle.
RECEPTIONIST	(to Intercom) Mr Watt. There's a Mr Little to see you.
MR LIDDLE	Er – excuse me. Not Little – Liddle.
RECEPTIONIST	Oh, I'm so sorry. (to Intercom) There's a Mr Liddle to see you, Mr Watt.

Dialogue 2

MR LIDDLE	Good morning.
MR WATT	Good morning. Please sit down. Now, what can I do for you?
MR LIDDLE	Well, my brother works in your accounts department and he suggested I came to see you. I understand you're looking for a junior clerk to join the firm.
MR WATT	That's not quite right. We're looking for a senior clerk as a matter of fact – one who has had experience of our kind of business.

Dialogue 3

MR WATT	What kind of experience have you had?
MR LIDDLE	Well (clears throat) I've just left school. Er – I haven't had a job before.
MR WATT	Well, I'm afraid your brother has made a mistake. We haven't any vacancies for school leavers at the moment. Sorry I can't help you.

B Dialogue 4

PHILIPS	Philips speaking.
CALLER	Good morning. My name is and I have an account with your company.
PHILIPS	Sorry. I didn't catch your name.
CALLER	Knapp. John Knapp.
PHILIPS	Can you spell that please?
CALLER	K-N-A- double P.
PHILIPS	K-N-A- double P?
KNAPP	Yes.

Dialogue 5

(Still on the telephone)

PHILIPS Yes, Mr Knapp.
KNAPP I have an account with your company and I received a bill from you today for £599.43. But in fact I think it's a mistake because according to our accounts we owe you only £499.43.
PHILIPS We sent you a bill for £599.43?
KNAPP Yes, that's right.
PHILIPS And how much did you think you owed us?
KNAPP £499.43.
PHILIPS £499.43?
KNAPP Yes.
PHILIPS What is the invoice number, please?
KNAPP 4107751.
PHILIPS 410...?
KNAPP 7751.
PHILIPS 4107751. I'll look into it right away, Mr Knapp. And I'll call you back.
KNAPP Thank you, Mr Philips.

ANSWERS TO LISTENING EXERCISE

A

Dialogue 1	Liddle	✓
	Little	
Dialogue 2	a junior clerk	
	a senior clerk	✓
Dialogue 3	The company	can offer the young man a job	
		cannot offer the young man a job	✓

B

Dialogue 4   KNAPP

Dialogue 5   i) £599.43

　　　　　　　ii) £499.43

　　　　　　　iii) 4107751

---

3 Controlled Practice

A The statements may be corrected in a number of ways using phrases given in the Presentation section of the Unit. The words in italics in the suggested answers below should be spoken with greater emphasis as they carry the correct information.

1 No, that's not right. The time in New York is only *four* hours behind Greenwich Mean Time.

2 No, not Sweden. *Norway* has many oilfields in the North Sea.

3 That's not quite right. Concord flies from France to *Brazil*.

4 I'm afraid you've made a mistake. Marseilles is the biggest port in the *South of France*.

5 No, that's not quite right. The national language of Brazil is *Portuguese*.

6 No! not in the Indian Ocean. Tahiti is in the *Pacific* Ocean.

7 I'm afraid you've made a mistake. The lira is the currency of *Italy*, not Spain.

8 That's not quite right. Lombard Street is the centre of English *banking*.

TAPESCRIPT FOR CONTROLLED PRACTICE B

1 'Good morning. My name's Fogg.'
'Fogg. F-O- double G.'

2 'My address is 42 Thames Street.'
'42 Thames Street. That's T-H-A-M-E-S. Thames Street.'

3 'My phone number is 67451.'
'67451.'

4 'I work for Lloyds.'
'Lloyds. Double L-O-Y-D-S.'

5 'I'll be in London on 15th June.'
'15th June.'

6 'I'm travelling on the 8.45 train from York, which arrives at 10.55 a.m.'
'The 8.45 from York – It arrives at 10.55 a.m.'

7 'I'm staying at the Dorchester.'
'The Dorchester. D-O-R-C-H-E-S-T-E-R.'

8 'I'll be in London for 4 or 5 days.'
'4 or 5 days.'

9 'I'll be travelling with my colleague, Mr. Clark.'
'My colleague, Mr. Clark, C-L-A-R-K.'

10 'My room number is 427.'
'427.'

B Possible phrases for checking information:

1 Sorry, I didn't quite catch your name.
2 Can you repeat that please?
3 67 . . . ?
4 Can you spell that please?
5 15th June?
6 You are travelling on . . . ?
7 Sorry, I didn't quite catch the name.
8 You'll be in London for . . . ?
9 Can you repeat that please?
10 427?

The information you should have noted:

Fogg.

42 Thames Street.

67451.

Lloyds.

15th June.

The 8.45 from York, arrives 10.55 a.m.

The Dorchester.

4 – 5 days.

My colleague, Mr Clark.

427.

4 Transfer

Information Sheet B

MEXICO Facts and Figures

Area 1 769 183 square kilometres

Population (1970) 48 377 363

Geography mountainous with desert in the South.

Politics Mexico is a federal republic. There are 31 states.

Economy the most important exports are cotton, sisal, gold, silver, oil.

Industries there are several large oil refineries and a petrochemical complex at Cocoleasaque; tourism is also important and there is rapidly expanding consumer goods industry.

Mexico City the capital of Mexico and the largest city in North America.
altitude: 2278 metres
population: (1970) circa 6 874 165
climate: average maximum temperature 80.3 F (May)
average minimum temperature 11.9 C (December)
average rainfall 587 millimetres per year – dry in summer, wet in winter.

Unit 5 Requesting action

1 Listening

TAPESCRIPT

JACKSON Hello, Helen, is that you?
HELEN Er – Yes.
JACKSON Ah good. I found you at home. Listen. This really is very urgent. I have a meeting this afternoon and I need some information which is in File No. 125/CIF. Can you find it for me please –
HELEN But, Mr...
JACKSON – and can you send a telex right away with all the most important facts –
HELEN Mr Jackson!
JACKSON – and then could you copy the contents of the file and post the copies to me by express mail. Would you do that right away, please?
HELEN Mr Jackson. I'm very sorry, I can't.
JACKSON Can't? Why not?
HELEN I'm in bed, Mr Jackson.
JACKSON In bed! Good Heavens, are you ill?
HELEN No. It's 3 o'clock in the morning!
JACKSON Is it really? I'm terribly sorry. I completely forgot the time difference. Well, would you mind doing all those things in the morning? I mean as soon as you get to the office – please?
HELEN Yes, of course, Mr Jackson.
JACKSON Thank you so much. I'm grateful to you. And I'm so sorry I disturbed your sleep.
HELEN It's all right.
JACKSON Er – have a good night.
HELEN Thanks very much, Mr Jackson.

ANSWERS TO LISTENING EXERCISE

What does Mr Jackson ask Helen to do?	Can she do them right away?
1 Find the information in File No. 125/CIF.	No
2 Send a telex with the most important facts.	No
3 Copy the contents of the file.	No
4 Post the copies to Mr Jackson by express mail.	No

(She can't do any of these things because it is 3 o'clock in the morning.)

3 Controlled Practice

A Any of the forms given in the Presentation can be used.

Possible answers are:

1 Can you (please) speak up (please)?
2 Could you say that again, please?
3 Would you lend me your pen, please?
4 Could you tell me where the canteen is, please?
5 Would you mind sending me a telex to confirm that, (please)?
6 Can you let me know what happens, (please)?
7 Would you phone me back in half an hour, (please)?
8 Would you mind driving me to the station, (please)?
9 Can you pass me the telephone directory, (please)?
10 Could you give me some change for the telephone, (please)?

B Any of the forms given in the Presentation may be used. Possible answers are:

1 As in the example.

2 Request Could you reserve a room for me at the Meridian Hotel for Thursday and Friday?
  Response That's not possible I'm afraid.

3 Request Can you get 2 tickets for the theatre for Saturday night?
  Response I'll do it right away.

4 Request Would you mind phoning the office and telling them I'll be late?
  Response Certainly.

5 Request Could you tell Mr James I'd like to see him, please?
  Response Yes, of course.

6 Request Would you fetch me a timetable, please?
  Response I'm sorry I can't.

7 Request Could you make me a photocopy of this document, please?
  Response I'll do it right away.

8 Request Can you go and see if Mr Philips has arrived yet, please?
  Response Yes, of course.

9 Request Would you mind bringing me some more letter paper?
  Response I'm sorry I can't.

10 Request Would you please empty the waste-paper basket?
   Response That's not possible, I'm afraid.

---

4 Transfer

Student B
Respond to Student A's request. You are the Marketing Manager and are willing to help out wherever possible. However, you cannot change any of your own business appointments.

Mon	am	see design dept. about new brochure
	pm	meeting with Development, 2.30
Tues	am	
	pm	Departmental meeting on marketing budget
Wed	am	
	pm	Day off. Take children to the zoo.
Thurs	am	visit printers to discuss brochure 10.00 – 11.00
	pm	quarterly sales forecast to prepare
Fri	am	complete quarterly sales forecast
	pm	round of golf with Bank Manager

Unit 6 Reviewing the interviewees

1 Listening

TAPESCRIPT

JOHN   Generally, I like the more experienced candidates. However, I'm afraid I didn't like Mr Brown at all. I just can't stand working with people like him. Of the other two candidates I think I preferred Smith to Jones. I quite liked his attitude and he seemed to have more to offer.

PETER   I wasn't particularly impressed by any of them and I'm not keen on giving the job to the best of a bad lot.

SUSAN   I didn't like Brown either, but I'm not sure I'd like to offer it to Smith – he really had very little experience. I was quite keen on Jones and certainly I'd rather he got the job than Smith, even if he didn't have exactly the right experience.

JOHN   Well, none of us seem very keen on any of these three candidates. Perhaps we should readvertise the post. It would be a pity since I hate spending time on recruitment.

SUSAN   Oh! I don't think we need to do that. It seems to be between Smith and Jones. Why don't we ask them back for another ten minutes. I'll do the interviewing. I quite enjoy it.

COMPLETED TABLE

	Mr Brown	Mr Smith	Mr Jones
John	✗	✓ ✽	✓
Peter	✗	✗	✗
Susan	✗	✗	✽

3 Controlled Practice

1 ...like/enjoy...

2 ...don't like...(or hate/can't stand...)

3 ...would prefer...

4 ...wouldn't like...

5 ...would rather...

6 ...would prefer...

7 ...would rather...

8 ...wouldn't like...

9 ...wouldn't like...

10 ...wouldn't like...

Unit 7 Allocating the budget

1 Listening

TAPESCRIPT

CHAIRPERSON Well, let's move on to Point 5 on the agenda – the allocation of the £60,000 donated by George Smethurst. We've had 5 proposals put forward, which you've all got on your agendas. Well, who'd like to start the ball rolling? Yes, Bill.

BILL Well, I think there are 2 key areas where improvements are really necessary and where I think we should spend the money. These are, firstly, office accommodation and the workshop. I'd like to suggest that the money be equally allocated between these two areas.

CHAIRPERSON Charles, I can see from your frown that you don't agree.

CHARLES It's not that I disagree entirely with what Bill has suggested. I think it's certainly a good idea to spend some of the money on improving the workshops – and I'm all in favour of that. But I don't think that office accommodation is a priority at the moment, and therefore I'm not really for spending money on that. What I do feel we should allocate the money to is improving the company's recreational facilities.

CHAIRPERSON Thanks, Charles. And what do you think, Mike?

MIKE Well, if you ask me, I don't think we need worry about either the workshops or the recreation area, and I am firmly against spending money on those 2 proposals. What I would like to see is something done about the canteen – and the food served in it.

CHAIRPERSON Mary, you look ready to say something.

MARY Yes. I can't possibly agree to Mike's proposal about the canteen. The food, in my opinion, is certainly adequate and I don't see why we need to spend any money on food. It's not intended to be a 3-star restaurant. If they don't like the food here, and remember it's subsidised by US, they can always make their own arrangements.
I'm inclined to agree with Bill – that we should spend the money on the workshops and the office accommodation.

CHAIRPERSON Thanks, Mary. Susan.

SUSAN I'm inclined to agree with Mary's idea about spending the money on the workshop, but I'm rather against improving office accommodation at the moment. Not that it doesn't need it. It does. But it's rather a luxury. Now you may think my ideas are rather bizarre, but I think we should seriously consider investing some of the money – perhaps in antiques or paintings. You may well smile, but a little outside investment will at least give us something to fall back on.

CHAIRPERSON Well I think the best thing to do now would be to vote on the issue. All those in favour of..........

COMPLETED TABLE

	Bill	Charles	Mike	Mary	Susan
office accommodation	✓	✗		✓	✗
workshop	✓	✓	✗	✓	✓
recreation area		✓	✗		
paintings/antiques					✓
canteen			✓	✗	

3 Controlled Practice

The answers given here do not represent all the possibilities.

Alternative answers should express the same strength of agreement or disagreement.

3 I entirely agree with you.

4 I don't think I'm really in favour of that.

5 I can't possibly agree to that.

6 You are probably right.

7 I absolutely agree.

8 That is perhaps a good idea.

9 Up to a point I'd agree with you, but.

10 I can't possibly agree to that.

Unit 8 Management qualities

1 Listening

TAPESCRIPT

INTERVIEWER In the second part of this interview I'd like to ask each of you in turn what you consider to be the three most important qualities for a good manager. Perhaps we could hear your ideas first, Mr Renolds.

RENOLDS Well, I think that at present the most important quality is the ability to deal with other people. I know we are a manufacturing industry, but I feel very strongly that we also have a great responsibility towards our personnel.
Secondly .... well, let me see. Yes, in my opinion the second most important quality must be the ability to talk to our personnel about their jobs, their futures, their problems, etc. To be able to relate to them, you know.
And thirdly ..... well ..... I suppose I'd put adaptability as the third most important quality. I think that fits in with the other two points I mentioned to give my idea of a good manager.

INTERVIEWER Well thank you for your opinions, Mr Renolds. Perhaps we could hear your views now, Mr Pritchard.

PRITCHARD Well, I consider the present situation requires a rather different approach to the whole question of management and therefore different qualities for managers.
I believe that a good manager is one who can persuade people that his way is right. Isn't that why he is a manager? Getting people to accept his decisions and to follow his leadership – that, in my view, is the mark of a good manager.
Secondly, I feel that he should be firm with his people – that's how they'll come to respect him.
And thirdly .... I'm of the opinion that he should be physically fit. In this day and age the pressures and strains are so great that only the fittest can survive, and those are the ones who should be the managers. Mentally competent – of course – but physically competent, also.

INTERVIEWER Well, thanks, Mr Pritchard.
Could we hear what you think, Mrs Stainton.

STAINTON Yes, certainly. I think my views probably represent a mixture or synthesis of my colleagues' opinions.
The most important quality is, in my opinion, the ability to think flexibly – to find new answers and new solutions.
Secondly, I feel that as managers we should be able to handle people, as I'm sure that for the company, good labour relations means a happy and secure future. But this doesn't mean that we should be too lenient nor too dogmatic.
No, the third quality should be, in my view, the ability to direct and control people effectively.

INTERVIEWER Well, thank you all for your opinions.

COMPLETED TABLE

	John Renolds	Mark Pritchard	Susan Stainton
Communicative skill	2		
Adaptability	3		
Creativity			1
Sensitivity to others	1		2
Stamina		3	
Foreign language skill			
Authority		2	
Leadership		1	3

3 Controlled Practice

The answers given here do not represent all the possibilities

2 Oh really? I'm convinced that they are too long.

3 Oh really? I'm inclined to think we should decrease it.

4 Oh really? In my opinion the most important quality is creativity.

5 Oh really? I definitely think we should review them fortnightly.

6 Oh really? I tend to think we are not spending enough.

7 Oh really? I'm inclined to think the Marketing Department needs reorganising.

8 Oh really? I think that the R and D Department should concentrate on developing better products.

9 Oh really? I'm inclined to think we should reject them.

10 Oh really? In my opinion we should slow it down.

11 Oh really? I really *do* think we should increase them (or it).

Unit 9 Pricing policy

1 Listening

TAPESCRIPT

SALES MANAGER	Right – we've got a problem. We have a showroom full of cars and now the manufacturers want us to take delivery of at least 12 new models. We haven't got the space so what are we going to do about getting rid of the old models?
SALESMAN 1	How about reducing the price of the old models by 10%: quite a few people would be attracted by that I imagine.
SALESMAN 2	It might be a good idea to keep the price as normal, but add extras to each car free of charge – you know, things like radios, digital clocks, spotlights and so on. Most buyers like to think they're getting something for nothing.
SALESMAN 1	Yes, all right. And what do you think about offering free petrol for say, 200 miles?
SALES MANAGER	I like the idea, but I suggest that you two work out the costs first. Don't let's give away too much.
SALESMAN 2	Don't you think we should also check around the other agents too? After all they may have customers waiting for old models and they could take some of ours.
SALES MANAGER	Yes, good idea. We could do that first.
SALESMAN 1	If the costs aren't too high, I think we should take a whole-page advert in the local paper.
SALES MANAGER	We could certainly do that. OK. Why don't you two prepare the figures for me and we'll meet again at 4.00 p.m.

SUGGESTIONS

1 reduce the price of old models by 10%

2 keep the same price but add free extras to each car

3 free petrol for 200 miles

4 salesmen work out the costs first

5 *not* give away too much

6 check around the other agents

7 take a whole-page advert in the local paper

3 Controlled Practice

2 I think we should diversify job responsibilities.

3 Don't you think we should increase short-term borrowing facilities?

4 Why don't we discuss a long-term overdraft scheme?

5 It might be a good idea to buy in bulk.

6 I suggest that we improve our forecasts.

7 How about employing more sales reps?

8 What do you think about increasing worker participation in decision-making?

Unit 10 Office Talk (1)

1 Listening

TAPESCRIPT

1 SECRETARY Excuse me, Mr Bigg. My husband is ill at home. Do you mind if I leave early today?
   BIGG What time do you want to leave?
   SECRETARY Er – four o'clock?
   BIGG All right.

2 BOSS Now then Andrews. What news is there on this £60,000 contract?
   ANDREWS Er – er – may I smoke, Sir?
   BOSS No you may not. Just tell me the news!

3 PASSENGER (on train) Er – excuse me. Can I look at your newspaper? If you've finished with it, that is.
   SECOND PASSENGER Yes, of course.

4 PERSON A Good. Well that's settled. Let's go and discuss the details over some lunch.
   PERSON B Good idea.
   PERSON C Well, do you mind if I don't join you for lunch? I have something rather urgent to attend to.
   PERSON A But of course you must join us. What could be more urgent than the matter we have to discuss, eh?

5 FERGUSON Come in!
   SECRETARY Sorry to interrupt, Mr Ferguson. Can I take the invoices now?
   FERGUSON Hmm. Go ahead.

6 JONES It's like this, you see. I've had all Miss Blake's work to do because she's been ill this week, and there's the problem of the stoppages on the production line to attend to and...
   BOSS And you haven't finished your report yet?
   JONES That's right, Sir. Er – may I have another two days?
   BOSS Well OK.

7 JONES You know the conference that's being held at Brighton next week. Well, as you know, I'm very interested in that area, and I'd very much like to go. Do you mind if I have a couple of days off?
   BOSS No, I'm sorry. I can't allow that. There's too much to do here at the moment. We just can't spare you.

8 PERSON A Do you mind if I use your phone?
   PERSON B I'd rather you didn't. I'm waiting for an important overseas call.

WAS PERMISSION GRANTED?

Dialogue 1 Yes
Dialogue 2 No
Dialogue 3 Yes
Dialogue 4 No
Dialogue 5 Yes
Dialogue 6 Yes
Dialogue 7 No
Dialogue 8 No

3 Controlled Practice

B Any of the forms given in the Presentation can be used.
Possible answers and responses

1 Do you mind if I open a window?
(Go ahead.)

2 May I borrow a chair from here?
(Yes of course.)

3 Do you mind if I smoke?   (I'd rather you didn't.)

4 Can I use your typewriter to type my report?
(Yes of course.)

5 Can I talk to you about an urgent matter?
(All right.)

6 Do you mind if I don't go to the conference?
(Of course you must go.)

7 May I see the report you have just written?
(No you may not.)

8 Can I borrow some money to buy lunch?
(Well OK.)

9 Do you mind if I make a phone call?
(Go ahead.)

10 Do you mind if I don't give you an answer immediately?   (No, all right.)
May I give you an answer this afternoon?
(Yes of course.)

Unit 11 Wages and prices

1 Listening

TAPESCRIPT

A The cycle is simply...prices increase, cost of living rises and naturally employees ask for wage increases to match cost of living increases.

B Certainly, that's the cycle, the question is...which stage opens the cycle – the increase in prices or the increase in wages? Let's look at Artex Ltd. At the moment, the employees are asking for a 19% increase. This figure is based on an estimate of the rate of inflation, in other words price increases for next year. In a way they are causing their estimate of 19% to be right.

A Are you suggesting that wage demands are the first stage in the cycle?

B Well, yes. I am giving one example of where, at this moment, wage increases are leading to price increases and so the cost of living is rising.

A Yes, but I can tell you of other companies where the employees base their wage demands on the previous year's inflation rate. For example, Efflon are negotiating a pay deal at the moment and are talking about an increase in the range of 10 to 12%. So, in this case, price increases are the first stage in the cycle.

NUMBERED CYCLES

Artex Ltd

(1) wages are increasing
(2) prices are increasing
(3) cost of living is rising

Efflon Ltd

(1) prices are increasing
(2) cost of living is rising
(3) wages are increasing

3 Controlled Practice

1 ...lead to...
2 ...are causing...
3 ...are complaining...
4 ...help...
5 ...encourage...
6 ...is dropping.

7 ...are increasing...
8 ...rise...
9 ...means...
10 ...are doing...
11 ...are trying...
12 ...are not analysing....

4 Transfer

A *Student B*

Listen to Student A's description of the sales pattern for Artex Ltd's four major products in an average year. Use the information to plot the figures on the graph below.

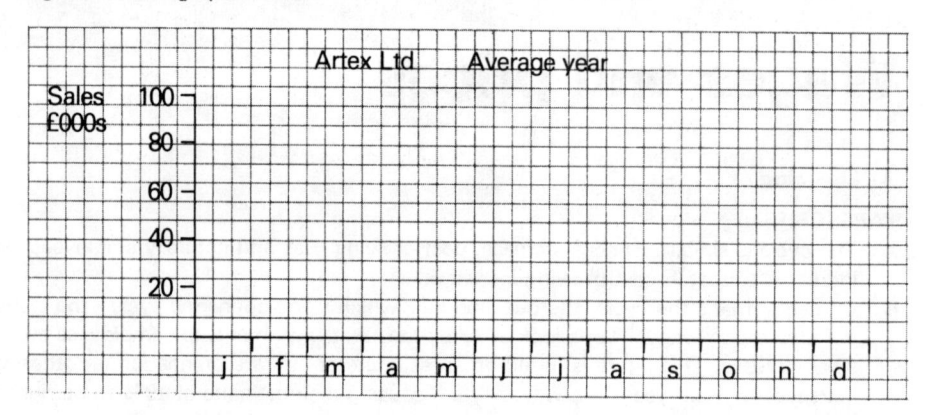

Artex Ltd   Average year
Sales £000s (0–100) vs months j f m a m j j a s o n d

B Now use the graph below to describe the sales situation at the moment for the four major products. Student A will plot this on his own graph.

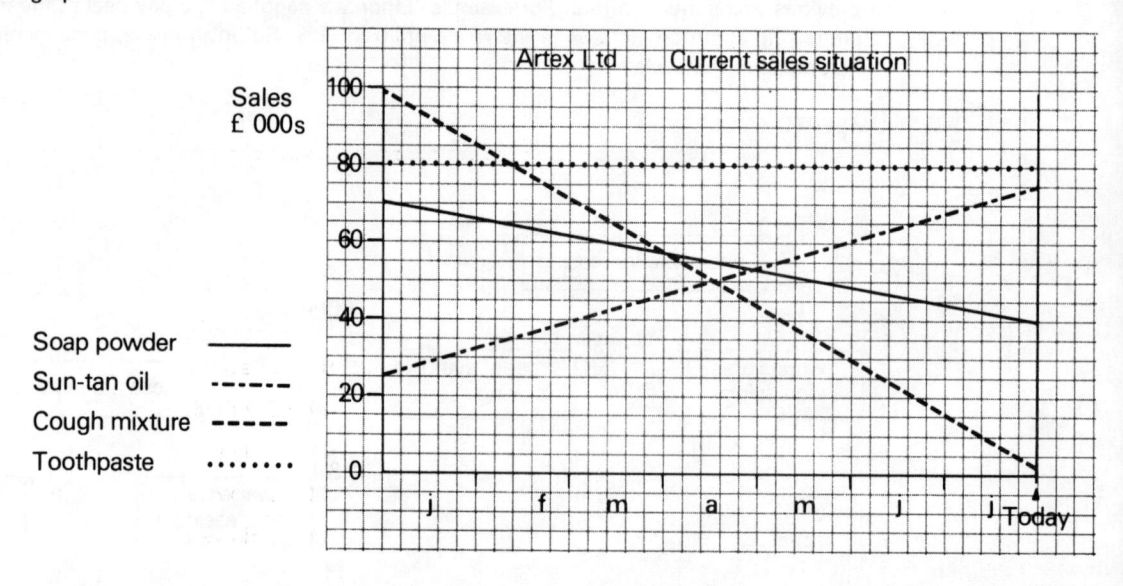

Artex Ltd   Current sales situation
Sales £ 000s vs months j f m a m j j Today

Soap powder ———
Sun-tan oil –·–·–
Cough mixture – – – –
Toothpaste ········

Unit 12 Travel expenses

1 Listening

TAPESCRIPT

FINANCE MANAGER	How did you get from London to Amsterdam?
SALESMAN	I flew, of course – from Gatwick.
FINANCE MANAGER	What time did you arrive?
SALESMAN	About 6 o'clock.
FINANCE MANAGER	Where did you stay?
SALESMAN	At the Grand Hotel.
FINANCE MANAGER	Did you eat out?
SALESMAN	Yes, I went to a restaurant nearby.
FINANCE MANAGER	How much did that cost?
SALESMAN	Oh, the equivalent of about £15.
FINANCE MANAGER	What time was your meeting the next day?
SALESMAN	At 11.
FINANCE MANAGER	So, how did you spend the morning?
SALESMAN	Well, I read over the report and then took a short walk through the centre of Amsterdam.
FINANCE MANAGER	How long did the meeting last?
SALESMAN	Well, we finished at 6.
FINANCE MANAGER	So you caught the next evening plane back to London?
SALESMAN	No, actually I slept another night at the Grand Hotel.
FINANCE MANAGER	Oh! so you came back the next morning?
SALESMAN	Yes, that's right. I managed to get the 8 o'clock plane.
FINANCE MANAGER	So, in all you had two nights in a first class hotel for one afternoon meeting.

VERB ORDER

to arrive	(3)	to finish	(13)	to manage	(17)
to be	(8)	to fly	(2)	to read	(10)
to catch	(14)	to get	(1)	to sleep	(15)
to come	(16)	to go	(6)	to spend	(9)
to cost	(7)	to have	(18)	to stay	(4)
to eat	(5)	to last	(12)	to take	(11)

---

3 Controlled Practice

1 ...went...
2 ...had...
3 ...wrote...
4 ...read...
5 ...met...
6 ...spent...
7 ...ate...
8 ...caught...
9 ...stayed...
10 ...visited...
11 ...flew...
12 ...saw...
13 ...drove...

1 Where did you have lunch?
2 Which report did you write up?
3 Did you finish the monthly sales report?
4 Did the plane arrive on time?
5 When did the departmental meeting finish?
6 What did you eat for lunch?
7 Did the plane leave on time?
8 Did you sleep well?
9 Which exhibition did you visit?
10 Did you have a good flight?
11 Why did you see the financial director?
12 Why did you drive to Manchester?

4 Transfer

Student B
Use the diary entries below to answer Student A's questions about last week's sales trip.

Monday	10.00 fly to Dijon 12.00 meet Mr. Jones 13.00 lunch at La Casserole 16.00 visit chemicals factory 19.00 train to Marseilles 21.00 arrive Marseilles
Tuesday	10.00 see main distributor 12.00 make presentation to the directors 14.00 taxi to Nice 17.00 arrive Nice 19.00 dinner with agent.
Wednesday	10.00 appointment at suppliers company. meet Leclerc and discuss pricing arrangements 12.00 catch plane to London 15.00 land in London

Unit 13 Work routines

1 Listening

TAPESCRIPT

SALES MANAGER   Well, I usually work in my office, of course. I spend a lot of time on the telephone and dealing with the post. I have to report to the General Manager every day to tell him what I am doing and why. I also have to meet the Finance Manager — twice a week — to discuss figures. The sales figures from each of our branches come in monthly, so every month, I have to check them very carefully to see if we have reached our targets. If we are below target, as happens sometimes, then I visit the branch and talk to the Branch Manager about it. I occasionally travel abroad too, when we have international Trade Fairs or important meetings with our parent company.

INTERVIEWER   Do you ever meet the customers themselves?

SALES MANAGER   Oh yes. Quite often. The important customers, such as the Government, always deal directly with myself.

INTERVIEWER   What else do you do?

SALES MANAGER   Well, there are the quarterly financial reports to prepare, and once a year we have our Annual General Meeting where we discuss the past year and fix the targets for the next year.

INTERVIEWER   How often do the company's annual sales figures fall below target?

SALES MANAGER   Oh, never!

COMPLETED TABLE

Activities	Frequency
1 work in the office	usually
2 have meetings with the Finance Manager	twice a week
3 report to the General Manager	every day
4 check the sales figures from all the branches	monthly/every month
5 visit other branches	sometimes
6 travel abroad	occasionally
7 prepare financial reports	quarterly/every three months
8 meet customers	quite often
9 deal with important customers	always
10 fix targets for the coming year	once a year

Answer to the question: Never.

3 Controlled Practice

A The missing words are:

1 monthly
2 quarterly; every three months
3 yearly/annual
4 twice a month

B The numbers could be expressed as:

1 – never
2 – occasionally
3 – sometimes
4 – quite often
5 – often

examples:
Businessmen never buy Nutto
Policemen occasionally buy Nutto
School children sometimes buy Nutto
etc.

Unit 14   Company rules and regulations

1 Listening

TAPESCRIPT

PERSONNEL MANAGER   Good morning, I'd like to welcome you to our organisation. Now you all know which departments you are going to, but before you go off I'm going to tell you a little bit about us and about the rules and regulations which we try to adhere to. And the reason why we have these rules is that they help us all to know what we can do, what we must do and what we shouldn't do – and in the long run make this a happy place to work.

First of all the flexitime system. Most of you can choose what time you are going to start and finish. However, you must all be here for core time which is from 10 till 3. You should all work for a minimum of 37 hours a week and normally you shouldn't work more than 41 hours. If you look at your job descriptions you'll see that you should put in an average of 38½ hours a week. This means you can put in up to an extra 2½ hours per week. However, at the end of a month you shouldn't have more than 10 hours overtime, because only 10 hours can be claimed. Is that clear?

As far as your daily working hours are concerned, you should tell the departmental heads on the Friday what times you are going to start the following week. You needn't start each day at the same time, but you must be here between 10 and 3, and you mustn't put in less than 37 hours in a week. And one more point, you needn't specify in advance what time you are going to finish.

You all have 18 days holiday a year. Ten of these 18 days must be taken during July when the company will be closed. The other eight days may be taken in either one or two instalments, for example five days and three days or six days and two days, etc. But you can't have eight separate single days off or four 2-day periods off.

We have a canteen here where you can have lunch. Lunch tickets are on sale on Monday mornings only and this means you must buy your tickets then for the rest of the week. The canteen is open between 12.30 and 2 o'clock and there are two sittings. You should decide on Monday which sitting you are going to attend and tell the supervisor when you buy your tickets.

So, any questions about these three points – flexitime, holidays and lunch – before I move on to the next matter.

COMPLETED TABLE

The secretaries:	TRUE	FALSE
may choose what time to start work	✓	
needn't work between 10 and 3		✓
mustn't work less than 37 hours a week	✓	
can claim a maximum of 10 hours overtime per month	✓	
should inform their department heads each Monday of their weekly hours		✓
must start each day at the same time in any one week		✓
needn't say in advance what time they intend to finish	✓	
can take 8 days holiday in July		✓
can take lunch in the canteen	✓	
must buy lunch tickets on Friday for the following week		✓

3 Controlled Practice

2a To arrive next day a letter must be posted before 4 p.m.
  b It shouldn't be used for sending valuable documents.
  c It needn't be posted in a post-office.

3a To arrive next day printed paper can't/mustn't be posted after 9.30 a.m.
  b It can/may be used for sending newspapers.
  c It needn't be posted in a post-office.

4a To arrive next day registered mail mustn't/can't be posted after 5 p.m.
  b It should be used for sending valuable written documents.
  c It can't/mustn't be posted in a post-box.

5a To arrive next day a package must be posted before 1 p.m.
  b It needn't be used for sending newspapers.
  c It must be posted in a post-office.

6a To arrive next day a parcel mustn't/can't be posted after 12 a.m.
  b It must be used for sending goods weighing more than 2 kg.
  c It can't/mustn't be posted in a post-box.

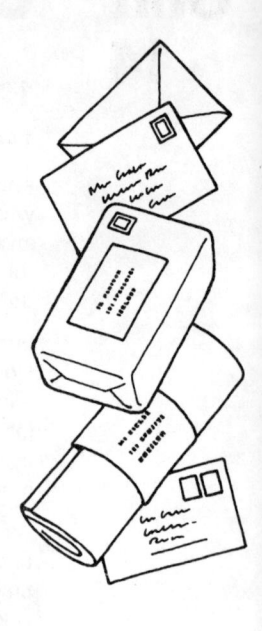

Unit 15 Plans and strategies

1 Listening

TAPESCRIPT

SALES MANAGER	Look, it's obvious. If we increase sales, we'll make a profit; and if we want to increase our sales, we'll have to increase our spending on advertising.
FINANCE MANAGER	No, you're absolutely wrong. We haven't got the money to increase our spending on advertising. If we increased our spending and still our sales didn't go up, we would be in serious financial difficulties. We should think about reducing our costs. If we reduced our spending on advertising and on other things, then we'd be in a stronger position.
PRODUCT MANAGER	I think what we need is a new product. The products we are selling now are becoming old-fashioned. No one wants to buy them. If we introduced a more up-to-date product we'd be more competitive.
FINANCE MANAGER	But we haven't got the money to back a new design.
GENERAL MANAGER	Gentlemen, please! Let's not talk about 'if we did this such and such would happen'. Let's think of the real possibilities. Now what about the contract with Harris. Are we going to get it?
SALES MANAGER	I think – if I go and see Harris tomorrow and make him a good offer, we'll get the contract. If we delay, we'll be too late.
GENERAL MANAGER	Well, if we can get the contract, we'll have some profit in hand. So, go ahead and make him the offer. Then we'll discuss our advertising situation.

COMPLETED FLOW DIAGRAM

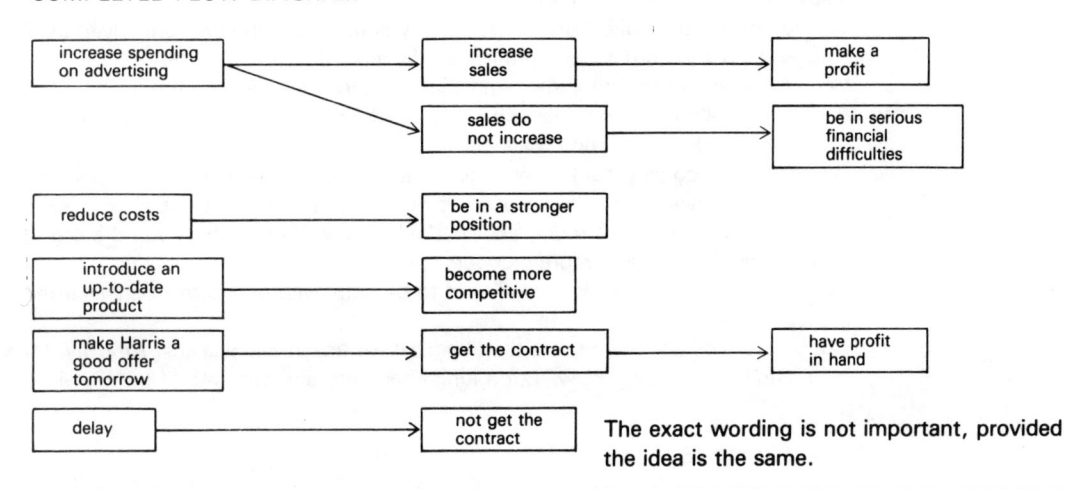

increase spending on advertising → increase sales → make a profit
                                 → sales do not increase → be in serious financial difficulties

reduce costs → be in a stronger position

introduce an up-to-date product → become more competitive

make Harris a good offer tomorrow → get the contract → have profit in hand

delay → not get the contract

The exact wording is not important, provided the idea is the same.

3 Controlled Practice

A Check your answers against the tapescript. See that you used the same forms of the conditional in each case.
i.e. If + present tense + future
or   If + past tense + conditional (with would)

B 1 If we get the contract, it will give us money to spend on advertising.

2 If we spent the profit on advertising, we'd lose it.

3 If we spent it on capital investment, it would provide some strength against inflation.

4 If we don't increase our market share now, we'll go into a decline.

5 If we increased our market share, we'd still need to invest.

6 If we beat our competitors now, our figures will rocket next year.

7 If our figures rocket, I'll be able to retire!

Unit 16 Interview preparations

1 Listening

TAPESCRIPT

SW Stuart Wilkinson, here.
PM Stuart, this is Paul McIntyre.
SW Well, what can I do for you, Paul?
PM You know these interviews which are scheduled for this afternoon?
SW Yes.
PM Well, have you read the CV's of the applicants? You see, I'm really busy at the moment and I just haven't got the time to study them in detail. I looked at them briefly yesterday and made a few notes, but you know the way I make notes!!
SW Yes, I certainly do! Anyway, hang on a minute and I'll get my notes.
SW Are you there?
PM Yes.
SW Well, first there's John Stevens.
PM He's the chap who worked for Chemico, isn't he?
SW Yes, that's right.
PM Chemico, Chemico. Who on earth are Chemico?
SW Chemico's the company which makes Kolopex.
PM Oh yes, of course. And Kolopex is the product we use in our paints.
SW No, no, you've got it all wrong. Kolopex is the product we add to our fertilizers.
PM Oh yes, of course. Anyway, what about the next applicant — Peter Murray, isn't it? Isn't he the fellow who was employed by Pharmico?
SW Wrong again, I'm afraid, Paul. Peter Murray is the man who was employed by Plastico.
PM And Plastico's the organisation that manufactures Biofin.
SW Well that one you should know. And Biofin is the preservative we put in our alcohol.
PM Right. What about the next candidate — Harold Harper? I can't remember anything at all about him.
SW Well, he was the Production Manager for Agrico.
PM Ah yes, it's all coming back now. And Agrico's the company that produces Pirone.
SW Nearly right. Pivone, not Pirone. And Pivone is the additive we put in our paint. Right?
PM Right. Anyway, only one more, and that's Anthony Short. I think you'd better give me his details so that I don't make any more blunders.
SW Yes, well, Short is the fellow who used to be employed by Pharmico. That's the company that makes Germitex.
PM Ah, yes, of course. Germitex is the chemical we use in our plastics. Anyway, thanks for your help, Stuart. Must rush now. Got a lunch appointment with one of the bigwigs!

COMPLETED TABLE

Name	Previous company	Company product	Product use
John Stevens	Chemico	Kolopex	fertilizers
Peter Murray	Plastico	Biofin	alcohol
Harold Harper	Agrico	Pivone	paint
Anthony Short	Pharmico	Germitex	plastics

3 Controlled Practice

1 the place where/where

2 the person who/the person that

3 the place where/where

4 cards which/cards that/devices which/devices that

5 the person who/the person that/who

6 a gate which/a gate that/a device which/a device that

7 when/a situation when

8 a device which/a device that/a bell which/a bell that

9 the person who/the person that/the one who/the one that

10 the place where/where

---

4 Transfer

A *Student B*

Answer Student A's questions about the subsidiaries of Trends UK Ltd for which you are area manager. Use the information in the table below to define the subsidiaries in terms of their products and their managers.

e.g. Trends Preston? That's the place where they produce raincoats.
The manager is Arthur Clark. He's the guy who used to be manager in Doncaster.

Subsidiary	Product	Manager Name	Previous post
Trends Swindon			
Trends Rochdale			
Trends Burnley			
Trends Bradford			
Trends Preston	raincoats	Arthur Clark	manager, Doncaster
Trends Blackburn	skirts	Jill Roberts	manager, Rochdale
Trends Doncaster	dresses	Margaret Lloyd	sales manager, Rochdale
Trends Wakefield	sportswear	Mary Duncan	sales rep., southern region

B Now ask Student A to give you information about the subsidiaries in his area. Ask him to define the subsidiaries in terms of
i their products
ii their managers

e.g. Tell me about Trends Swindon.
    What about the manager?

Use the information to complete your table above.

Unit 17 Sales call

1 Listening

TAPESCRIPT

SALESMAN	Good afternoon. I'm from Cookrite Ltd. We are leading manufacturers of microwave ovens. I wonder if I could take a few minutes of your time to tell you about our product?
COMPANY REP	I'm sorry but this is a pharmaceuticals company. Could you tell me what interest your microwave ovens are to us?
SALESMAN	Well, could I start by asking if you have a canteen here for your staff?
COMPANY REP	Yes, we do. A small one, but it's enough.
SALESMAN	How many staff do you have here?
COMPANY REP	About 150.
SALESMAN	And that includes pharmacists, lab. technicians, admin. staff and so on?
COMPANY REP	Yes, that's right.
SALESMAN	You are a long way from any town or village here, aren't you?
COMPANY REP	Er, yes. It's about three miles to Axton.
SALESMAN	So it's a long way for your staff to go to a restaurant or to go home for lunch, isn't it?
COMPANY REP	Yes, it is.
SALESMAN	So, most of them eat here – in the canteen. Is that right?
COMPANY REP	Some of them bring sandwiches.
SALESMAN	Are your staff happy with the canteen, do you think?
COMPANY REP	I – suppose so.
SALESMAN	Do you eat there yourself?
COMPANY REP	Well, sometimes. I must say, I prefer to drive into Axton if I have time.
SALESMAN	So you don't really enjoy eating there, do you?
COMPANY REP	Well –
SALESMAN	Why is that?
COMPANY REP	Well, there isn't any choice of dishes in the canteen. The kitchen isn't big enough to make a lot of different dishes, so they just make one dish each day – and sometimes it's something I don't like.
SALESMAN	If you had a choice of several dishes, you would be happy to eat more often in the canteen, is that right?
COMPANY REP	Yes – I suppose I would.
SALESMAN	And the same would be true of your staff?
COMPANY REP	Maybe.
SALESMAN	You see, with our microwave ovens, a dish can be heated up in just a few seconds, so you can make a variety of dishes without a lot of pots and pans. And they take up much less space than a normal cooker, so you could put two or three into your small kitchen...

COMPLETED TABLE

TRUE/FALSE

1 TRUE   6 FALSE
2 TRUE   7 FALSE
3 TRUE   8 TRUE
4 FALSE   9 TRUE
5 FALSE   10 FALSE

3 Controlled Practice

Suggested answers

1 Could I start by asking you what your full company name is?
2 Could you tell me if it is a British owned company?
3 I wonder if you could tell me how many employees you have?
4 The main factory is situated near London, isn't it?
5 The chief company product is oil drilling meters, is that right?
6 Who do you sell to in the UK?
 (Could you tell me who you sell to in the UK?)
7 Which Middle East country is your main export market?
8 Are there any other important export markets?
 (Have you any other important export markets?)
9 You haven't any other distributors, have you?/is that right?
10 When can we visit your factory?
 (Could you tell me a suitable date when we can visit your factory?)

4 Transfer

Student B
Use the c.v. below to answer Student A's questions about your personal details, qualifications and experience.

Full name	Christopher John Baines
Date of birth	6.8.57 Age 24
Address	54 New Street, Birmingham
~~Single~~/Married/~~Divorced~~/~~Separated~~	
Children	John Anthony Age 2 years
Education	
1968 - 1975	Quinton Boys Grammar School, Birmingham
1975 - 1978	University of Manchester
Qualifications	
1975	A levels in Maths, Applied Maths, Physics and Statistics
1978	BSc Mathematics 2nd Class
Experience 1978 - present	Savings Bank, Birmingham Head Office Trainee computer programmer Worked entirely on COBOL but also familiar with BASIC and FORTRAN

Unit 18 Office Talk (2)

1 Listening

TAPESCRIPT

MANAGER   Come in, John. Have you finished that report for me yet?
JOHN   Yes, but I haven't had time to prepare the sales figures yet, I'm afraid.
MANAGER   That's all right, I know you've been busy. I believe you've just moved house.
JOHN   Not quite, we're moving next week. We've been in our present house since 1977 and it's got too small for us this last year or so.
MANAGER   Well, I hope the new place suits you better.
JOHN   I think it will. It's taken us six months to find a bigger place we like – one with a bigger garden. Since the children have grown they've needed a lot more space.
MANAGER   Well, the best of luck with the new place – I hope the move goes well.
JOHN   Thanks. Oh, by the way, I've sent a copy of the report to the Board – is that OK?
MANAGER   Yes, good idea. The Sales Director has just asked me about it in fact. They've already decided to accept whatever recommendations you've made, so they obviously trust your judgement.
JOHN   That's good. I'll go and make a start on the sales figures now then.
MANAGER   OK John. I'll see you later when you've finished them.

COMPLETED TABLE

	TRUE	FALSE
John has finished the report.	✓	
He hasn't done the sales figures yet.	✓	
John hasn't had much work.		✓
John has already moved house.		✓
He and his wife need a smaller place.		✓
The children want more space.	✓	
A copy of his report has gone to the Board.	✓	
The Board is going to decide whether to accept his report.		✓

3 Controlled Practice

3 The Company has already employed an American agent.

4 American dealers have shown interest in our products for the last two years.

5 We haven't signed contracts with American dealers yet.

6 Our MD has already visited New York.

7 The Marketing Department has carried out research since 1979.

8 The R & D Department has been working on a special product range for six months.

9 They've already come up with two new products.

10 We haven't studied the American regulations yet.

11 We have exported special products to other countries since 1978.

12 The Sales Department has already trained reps for the American market.

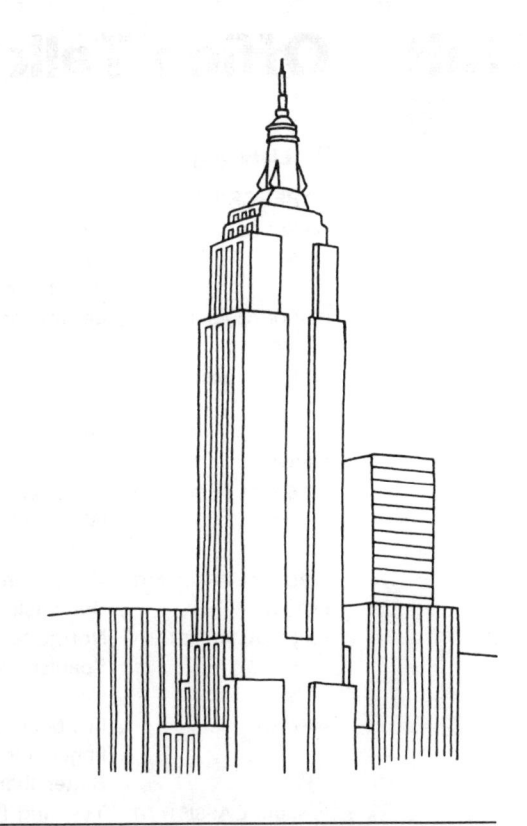

4 Transfer

Student B
Answer Student A's questions using the information below.

Sales Department

Items	Year 1 Plan	Actual
No. of new sales reps.	+2	+1
Sales target	£250,000	£245,000
New customers per sales rep.	+5	+3
Sales costs	-10%	-3%
Sales training (weeks)	20	15
Appointment of agents	+6	+2

Production Department

Items	Year 1 Plan	Actual
No. of employees	-5	-2
Production target (units)	+2,000	+1,800
New plant (machines)	+3	+4
Production costs	-10%	-6%
Training (weeks)	10	8

Unit 19 Office Talk (3)

1 Listening

TAPESCRIPT

PERSONAL ASSISTANT	Good morning, Mr Brown. Welcome back. How was your holiday?
BROWN	Well, apart from the weather, marvellous. But I suppose I shouldn't grumble. It didn't rain every day. Anyway, what's been happening in the office?
PERSONAL ASSISTANT	Let me look in the file .... Oh yes, three important things have happened.
BROWN	Uh-huh.
PERSONAL ASSISTANT	Firstly — we've had a bit of a shake-up over in the Marketing Department. Fairburn has been replaced by Taylor, and three new admin. posts have been created in the section.
BROWN	And what about Johnson?
PERSONAL ASSISTANT	I was just coming to him. When he heard about the changes, he resigned.
BROWN	Well, well, that *is* news. And what were the other two important things?
PERSONAL ASSISTANT	Well, there's a bit of a surprise for you, too.
BROWN	Don't tell me I've been put on a three-day week.
PERSONAL ASSISTANT	Not quite. You've been selected to go on an intensive language course in Spanish early next year. You'll be going to Barcelona for two weeks. Very nice, too.
BROWN	I've been waiting for that course since last year. About time they pulled their finger out in the Training Department. Um .... two weeks in Barcelona. Better than Blackpool, I suppose.
PERSONAL ASSISTANT	Yes, and finally the big Saudi deal came through last week. They accepted our terms completely. Pity you missed the celebratory party, though.

COMPLETED TABLE

	TRUE	FALSE
Mr Brown had good weather on his holiday.		✓
Nothing important has happened in the office.		✓
There have been a number of changes in the Marketing Department.	✓	
Taylor has taken over Fairburn's job.	✓	
Three new marketing posts have been created in the Marketing Department.		✓
Johnson decided to leave the company.	✓	
Mr Brown went to Barcelona for an intensive language course last year.		✓
The Saudi company rejected the terms offered by Mr Brown's company.		✓

3 Controlled Practice

1 we made
2 OK
3 we have had
4 OK
5 they were
6 we have been waiting/have waited
7 our Marketing Manager visited
8 OK
9 our policy has always been
10 OK

4 Transfer

Student B
Use the table below to reply to Student A's questions about changes in the office.

WHO	WHAT	WHEN	WHY
Max	Sacked	2 weeks ago	Stole company property
Sheila	Suspended	2 weeks ago	Aided Max
Peter	Sick	This week	Overworking
Fred	Getting on people's nerves	This week	Complaining about overwork
Julie	Handed in her notice	Last Friday	Found a better job
Clare	Seconded to Finance Dept.	This week & next week	Backlog of work

Unit 20 Past appointments, future engagements

1 Listening

TAPESCRIPT

TAYLOR   Oh, there you are, Carter. Come in and sit down.
CARTER   Thanks.
TAYLOR   Now then, have you been in touch with Mr Pearson yet?
CARTER   Yes. I talked to him yesterday afternoon. He's coming to the ITA meeting next week so you'll be able to talk to him yourself.
TAYLOR   Er – what day is the ITA meeting?
CARTER   It's on Tuesday, Mr Taylor.
TAYLOR   Ah good. I'm leaving for Paris on Thursday, so that gives me a free day before I leave. Now, before the meeting next week, you must have your sales figures ready. In fact, I'd like you to have them ready on Friday so that I can look at them at the weekend. Can you do that?
CARTER   Yes, Mr Taylor.
TAYLOR   And I'd also like to see the report on the Trade Fair that you went to last week.
CARTER   Yes, Mr Taylor.
TAYLOR   Do you happen to know when the marketing director will be back from the U.S.A.?
CARTER   Yes, he should be back tomorrow.
TAYLOR   Oh, good. The Board Meeting is the day after tomorrow. I must try to arrange to see him tomorrow afternoon. Could you be there too, do you think? You haven't got anything on tomorrow, have you?
CARTER   Well – I had arranged to see my doctor for a check-up. You know I had that accident last month – and just to make sure I'm OK...
TAYLOR   What time are you seeing the doctor?
CARTER   5 o'clock.
TAYLOR   Oh, that shouldn't cause any problem. Just leave when you have to.
CARTER   OK, that's fine. I'll get back to my office. Bye.
TAYLOR   Bye.

COMPLETED TIME-PLAN

last month	last week	this week			TODAY			week-end		next week					
		Sat	Sun	Mon	Tue	Wed	Thu	Fri	Sat	Sun	M	T	W	T	F	
						7	8					2		3		morning
									5 →							
10	6			1		9		4				2				afternoon
						11										
																evening

110

3 Controlled Practice

A Expanded telegrams

1 John will see you on Thursday at 4.30 (half past four) in the afternoon.

2 Miss Peabody is travelling to the USA on 31st May. She is returning in July.

3 Please phone Frank Martin between 9 and 10 on Friday morning.

4 David Simon can't make tonight. He suggests a meeting on Friday at 8 o'clock or at the weekend. Please phone him as soon as possible.

B 1 Mr Ferguson is retiring in ten days' time/next week.

2 I'm meeting Jane for lunch in an hour's time.

3 Mr Smith phoned an hour ago.

4 The last meeting was held two weeks ago.

5 Your letter arrived two days ago/the day before yesterday.

6 I returned from Rome last week/a week ago.

7 The report must be ready by tomorrow afternoon.

8 We are having dinner this evening.

4 Transfer

TIMETABLE for the Secretary's use only.

MON.	TUE.	WED.	THU.	FRI.
2 p.m. Appointment with Mr Baker 3 p.m. Meeting with Works Council	8 a.m. Train to London. 10.05 Arrive London 11 a.m. Meeting at Dorset Hotel 8 p.m. A.E.M. Dinner	10 a.m. Meeting with STN 12 a.m. Meeting with Mr Ray (and lunch) 3.30 p.m. See Mr. Tate 5 p.m. Train leaves (arrives 7.10)	No appointments 2 p.m. Meeting with Finance department.	9.30 a.m. Show Japanese visitors around department Lunch with Board of Directors

Unit 21 Making arrangements

1 Listening

TAPESCRIPT

PETER Is that you John?
JOHN Yes.
PETER This is Peter from Training. I wanted to talk to you about the language course we discussed the other day.
JOHN Oh yes, you mean the French one.
PETER It's just a matter of fixing a suitable week for you. How are you fixed up after the summer?
JOHN Hang on, let me just find my diary...OK. It looks as though I'm going to be pretty busy in the autumn.
PETER Right, the language school says that they can take you from Week 36 onwards but they need to know as soon as possible. What are you doing in Week 36?
JOHN Well, I'm flying out to Kuwait on the Monday to visit our subsidiary there...they've got a couple of problems at the terminal.
PETER When do you plan to be back?
JOHN I doubt if I'll be back before the weekend.
PETER I see, so that's a pretty important engagement.
JOHN Umh...the following week I'm going to work on my six-monthly report for the GM. That'll take me most of the week and when that's finished, I'm going to the Midlands to visit our distributors.
PETER Let's leave that week...what about week 38?
JOHN It's not fixed up yet but I think a study-group from Germany is going to visit us – in which case I aim to help out...the next fortnight – that's 39 and 40 – I'm spending in Miami on holiday.
PETER When do you get back?
JOHN Our flight leaves Miami on Friday. Then there's a trade fair in Switzerland for two days the following week. I'm not sure if I'm going to attend but I'd like to. It depends..., then in 42, I've our monthly meeting with the maintenance department and I also intend to finish the design plans for the Kuwait job that week.
PETER You're obviously going to be pretty busy. However, the language school needs to know if and when you are going to attend and they need to know by the end of the week. Could you please get back to me as soon as possible.
JOHN OK, I'll ring you back this afternoon.

COMPLETED ENGAGEMENTS PLAN

ENGAGEMENTS	WEEK NOS.
Finish design plans for Kuwait plant	42
Prepare 6-monthly report	37
Aid study-group visit	38
Trade fair in Switzerland	41
Visit Kuwait subsidiary	36
Holiday in Miami	39 and 40
Visit distributors in Midlands	37
Monthly meeting with Maintenance Dept.	42

3 Controlled Practice

A 2 I'm visiting HQ in Brussels.

3 I'm going to see the Marketing Manager.

B 1 Where do you plan to spend your holidays?

2 We're taking the train to Marseilles.

3 What on earth do you intend to do there?

4 We're not staying there.

C 1 When do you aim to have the report ready?

2 It'll be ready this afternoon.

Unit 22 Recruitment procedures

1 Listening

TAPESCRIPT

A Our personnel director has commented on how long our recruitment procedure for middle management takes. I'd like to spend a few minutes reviewing it and then perhaps we can look at ways it can be shortened. John, can you take us through the process as it stands?

B Yes, certainly. Once a position becomes vacant, the post is initially advertised internally. If there are no applicants from within the company, the post is then advertised in the national newspapers. Replies to this advertisement are assessed and the next step is to produce a short-list of suitable applicants. As soon as an interview panel has been selected, these candidates are invited to an interview. In most cases, two or three applicants come through this stage successfully and are then asked to attend a final interview. In the meantime, references are requested for these candidates. On the basis of the final interview and these references, one applicant is chosen. The job is then offered to this candidate and finally, he is invited for an informal discussion day prior to taking up the job.

A Thank you John. Perhaps we could now go through the process step by step and see if we can shorten or cut out any of these stages.

NUMBERED STAGES

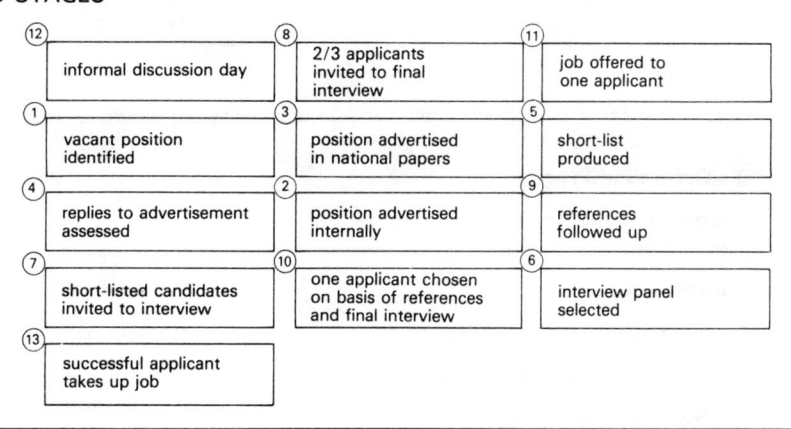

(12) informal discussion day	(8) 2/3 applicants invited to final interview	(11) job offered to one applicant
(1) vacant position identified	(3) position advertised in national papers	(5) short-list produced
(4) replies to advertisement assessed	(2) position advertised internally	(9) references followed up
(7) short-listed candidates invited to interview	(10) one applicant chosen on basis of references and final interview	(6) interview panel selected
(13) successful applicant takes up job		

3 Controlled Practice

1 Firstly/Initially/In the first place/To start with...

2 Then...

3 Prior to/Before...

4 Once...

5 Then...

6 Once/As soon as...

7 ...then...

8 Finally/Lastly...

9 ...before...

Unit 23 Deciding company policy

1 Listening

TAPESCRIPT

JOHN I think that what we must do now is concentrate our efforts on both the home and the foreign markets, and for that we've got to get extra capital from the bank. As a small company we are in a vulnerable position and I think we all realise that we mustn't only concentrate on the home market. However, we needn't increase our product range yet – that can wait. Another thing – we needn't grow very quickly – rather at a steady pace, I'd say – over the next few years, if we are going to survive.

PETER I'm a little worried about getting extra capital from the bank. I really don't think we need to borrow money at the moment. Our products have been very successful in this country and I think we are doing very well. We don't need to rush into the foreign market-place yet. I think we've got to concentrate just on the home market and stabilise our position here. And for that we've got to grow – but not very quickly or we'll explode.

MIKE I think I rather agree with you, John. We've got to be dynamic in our approach, and I think we must develop both the local and the foreign markets. But here I disagree with both of you. I think that if we are going to survive we've got to grow very quickly. By that I mean that we need to develop new products, and this of course means we've got to borrow capital from the bank.

COMPLETED TABLE

	✓	–	✗
concentrate only on the home market	P		J
concentrate only on the foreign market			
concentrate on both the home and foreign markets	J M		
borrow money from the bank	J M	P	
grow very quickly	M	J	P
increase product range	M	J	

---

3 Controlled Practice

The answers given here do not represent all the possibilities.

Company A

1 We must increase production.

2 We mustn't take on more staff.

3 We don't need to develop new products.

4 The French subsidiary must invest in new machinery.

5 We need to increase prices to the retailers.

6 The company doesn't need to spend more on advertising.

Company B

1 The company doesn't need to increase production.

2 The Production Department must take on more staff.

3 The Research Department must develop new products.

4 We don't need to invest in new machinery.

5 We mustn't increase prices to our retailers.

6 The Promotion Department must not spend more on advertising.

Unit 24 Product description

1 Listening

TAPESCRIPT

Gentlemen, today I'm going to introduce our new 1500 in the B range. This model will take over from the old B1368, which will not be produced after the end of this year.

If we compare the 1500 with the 1368 we notice a number of improvements in relation to its size, weight and performance. Let's first compare the dimensions of the 1500 and the 1368. The old model was 1000 mm long and we have reduced this to 900 mm. The width of the old model was 450 mm; the new model is 400 mm wide. Finally the old model was 800 mm in height and in the new model this has been reduced to 745 mm. Not exactly enormous modifications – but even a small reduction in size is an improvement.

We have also managed to reduce the weight. The new model weighs 238 kg compared to the old model's 252. Again a small improvement.

Of course the weight and the dimensions are not matters of the highest priority to our customers. They are interested in performance and it is in this area that we have concentrated most of our attention. The new model can turn out 350 units per minute, as against the old model's 250 per minute, and this is a big increase.

The final modification or rather improved feature that I shall mention is durability. We can now advise our customers that the machine need be serviced after 1800 hours use as compared to the recommended servicing every 1600 hours with the 1368.

Thank you, gentlemen, for your attention.

COMPLETED TABLE

	B1368	B1500
Length	1000 mm	900 mm
Width	450 mm	400 mm
Height	800 mm	745 mm
Weight	252 kg	238 kg
Performance (units per minute)	250 units	350 units
Service intervals	1600 hours	1800 hours

3 Controlled Practice

Length	Q	How long is it?
	A	It's 9 metres long.
Width	Q	How wide is it?
	A	It's 3 metres wide.
Height	Q	How high is it?
	A	It's 3 metres high.
Base Area	Q	What's its base area?
	A	It's 27 square metres.
Volume	Q	What's its volume?
	A	It's 81 cubic metres.
Load	Q	How much can it carry?
	A	It can carry 20 tons.
Capacity	Q	How many fridges can it hold?
	A	It can hold 80 fridges.

4 Transfer

Student B

You are a supplier of office furniture. Respond to Student A's requests for information about items of office furniture. Use the specifications below.

Coffee tables	Models A	L = 0.8m	W = 0.8m	H = 0.6m
	B	L = 1.2m	W = 1.2m	H = 0.6m
Office desks	Models A	L = 1.2m	W = 0.8m	H = 1.3m
	B	L = 1.5m	W = 0.8m	H = 1.3m
	C	L = 2.0m	W = 1.0m	H = 1.3m
Book-cases	Models A	L = 1.0m	W = 0.3m	H = 1.6m
	B	L = 1.5m	W = 0.3m	H = 1.6m
	C	L = 2.0m	W = 0.3m	H = 1.6m

(0.5m length holds 50 catalogues)

Filing cabinets	Models A	L = 0.6m	W = 0.7m	H = 1.6m
	B	L = 0.6m	W = 0.7m	H = 2.0m
Open-hanging filing systems	Models A	L = 0.5m	W = 0.5m	H = 0.7m
	B	L = 1.0m	W = 0.5m	H = 0.7m
	C	L = 1.5m	W = 0.5m	H = 0.7m
	D	L = 2.0m	W = 0.5m	H = 0.7m

(0.5m length holds 50 separate items)

Unit 25 Value, price and efficiency

1 Listening

TAPESCRIPT

ADVISER   Now the electric panel radiators are very good. They are clean, efficient and easy to adjust to the temperature you want.
Mr JAMES   How much does it cost to install them?
ADVISER   Well, they are quite cheap to install. For your premises, I should think they would cost between £5,000 and £6,000.
Mr JAMES   And what about running costs?
ADVISER   Well, quite expensive because they are electric. You should calculate on about 20p an hour for an average sized room.
Mr JAMES   Then we have the hot air vents. What do you think about those?
ADVISER   Well, these would be very expensive to install, of course, and the disadvantages are that you get very dirty walls and ceilings from them, and also they are less adjustable. You have to adjust the temperature at source – although individuals can shut off the vents in their offices if they wish.
Mr JAMES   Are they expensive to run?
ADVISER   That depends if the system is oil-fired or gas-fired. The gas-fired systems are quite cheap. Say about 8p an hour per room.
Mr JAMES   Gas heating is still the cheapest, isn't it?
ADVISER   Yes, it is at present. But it will become more expensive in the future. Now the gas-fired radiators are very good value. They are as good as the electric radiators in every way, and at present, they are cheaper to run.
Mr JAMES   How much per hour?
ADVISER   About 10p per hour per room.
Mr JAMES   And the cost of installation?
ADVISER   Well, it will cost a little more than the electric radiators because you have to install a boiler. Perhaps for you, about £10,000.
Mr JAMES   And what about the ceiling heating. That sounds like a good system.
ADVISER   Not really. You see, heat rises, so you lose most of your heating through the roof and your feet get cold! It's not very efficient. It is however, fairly cheap to install, perhaps about £5,000.
Mr JAMES   But more expensive to run because you lose heat?
ADVISER   Yes. You have to turn it to maximum to feel warm so you would spend as much as 40p per hour perhaps!
Mr JAMES   Yes, that's a lot!

COMPLETED TABLE

	electric panel radiators	hot air vents	gas-fired radiators	electric ceiling heating
How much does it cost to install?	£5,000–£6,000	very expensive	£10,000	£5,000
How much does it cost to run?	20p an hour (per average sized room)	8p an hour	10p an hour	40p an hour

3 Controlled Practice

Possible questions and answers

1 How much does it cost to fly from London to New York?
The normal excursion fare is £340.

2 How much is a Sunday newspaper in Britain?
Between 15 and 28p.

3 What's the price of a London theatre ticket?
About £5.

4 What's the cost of a telephone call from UK to France?
It costs 30p a minute.

5 How much do you pay for an apartment in London?
You pay about £100 a week or more.

6 How much are apples in Britain?
They are about 20p a pound.

7 What's the price of petrol in Britain?
It's £1.80 a gallon.

8 How much is a cup of coffee?
25p.

9 What do you pay for steak?
It costs £2 a pound.

10 How much does it cost to travel by train from London to Edinburgh?
It costs about £30.

11 How much are records?
They are about £5 each.

12 What is the price of land outside the city centre?
It's about £3,000 an acre.

4 Transfer

Student B
Use the information below to answer Student A's questions about price.

Furniture	
Settee	£300
Armchairs	£80 each
Double bed	£120
Single beds	£90 each
Wardrobe	£150 each
Chest of drawers	£130 each
Fridge	£80
Fridge freezer	£130
Freezer	£190
Dining table	£70
Dining chairs	£40 each

Clothes	
Lightweight suits	£120 each
Cotton shirts	£10 each
Cotton trousers	£20 each
Lightweight jacket (blazer)	£70
Shoes	£20 a pair

Unit 26 Inflation

1 Listening

TAPESCRIPT

Perhaps we could look briefly at the way inflation has developed during the period 1975 to 80 since this has certainly had an effect on our general performance. On the graph in front of you, the horizontal axis represents the years 75 to 80 divided up into six-monthly periods. The vertical axis shows the % rate of inflation from zero to 25. Let us now look in detail at the development......

If we start with 1975, you can see that at the beginning of the year, inflation stood at 5%. It increased steadily over the next 12 months to 8%. Things improved at the beginning of 1976 and it levelled off for a six-month period. The improvement continued and inflation decreased gradually by 2% during the rest of the year. Unfortunately, as you can see, the decline was not maintained and over the next six months inflation rose slightly and reached 9% by the middle of 1977. Then we hit a bad patch – I'm sure you will remember how inflation went up dramatically to 17% during the next 12 months and the effect this had on our exports. After a drop of 3% over the 2nd half of 78 when we all thought that things were improving, inflation increased rapidly until it reached a peak of 24% in mid-79. This marked the low point for us and the high point for inflation. It then fell to 20% by the end of 79 and subsequently levelled off until the middle of 1980. Now let's look at our results during this same period ......

COMPLETED GRAPH

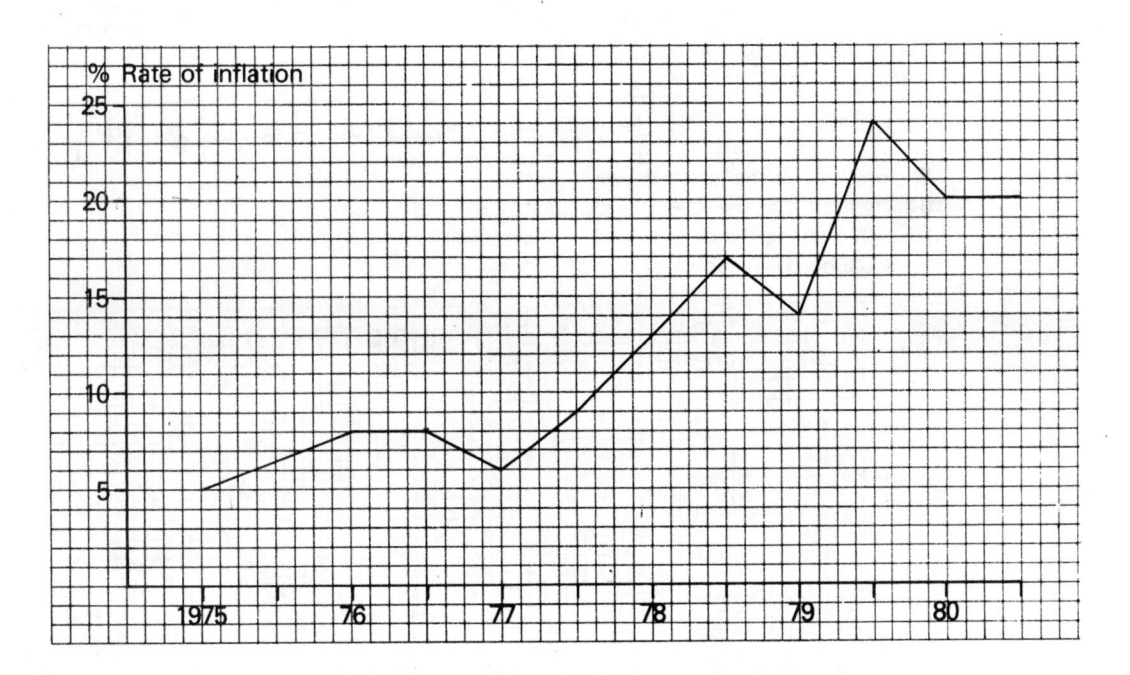

3 Controlled Practice

A
1b decreased/fell/dropped/went down.
2 levelled off.
3 increased/rose/went up.
4 reached a peak.
5 decrease/fall/drop.
6 rise.
7 levelled off.

B
1a at
1b to
2 at
3 by
4 of
5 to
6 of
7 at

4 Transfer

A *Student B*
Listen carefully to Student A's description of monthly ice-cream sales and use the information to complete the graph below.

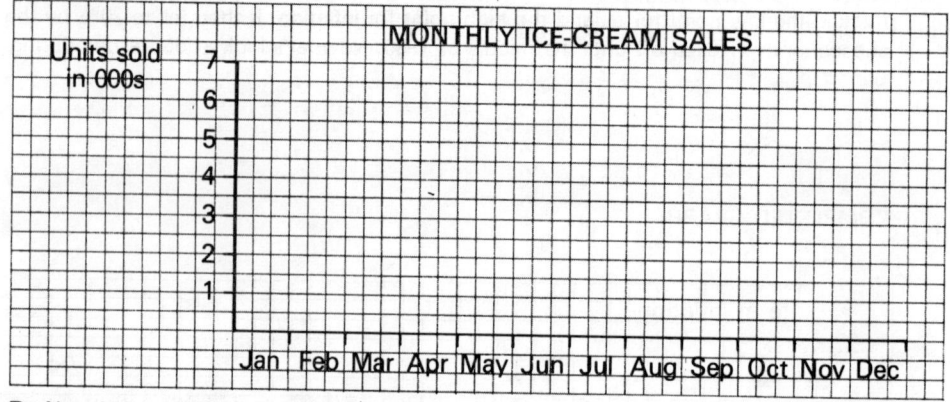

MONTHLY ICE-CREAM SALES
(Units sold in 000s, Jan–Dec, scale 1–7)

B Now look at the graph showing traffic density figures below. Describe the density of the traffic during the day to Student A who will complete his own graph.

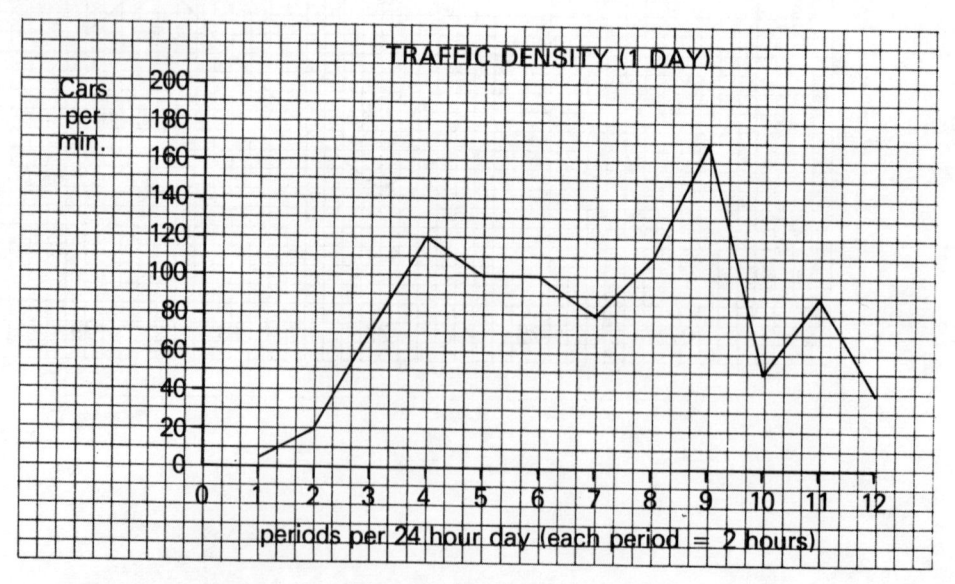

TRAFFIC DENSITY (1 DAY)
(Cars per min., 0–200; periods per 24 hour day (each period = 2 hours), 0–12)

Unit 27 Delivery dates

1 Listening

TAPESCRIPT

RECEPTIONIST	I'll just put you through to dispatch section.
ORDER CLERK	Dispatch section here.
KLINE	Morning, this is Mr Kline of D and Bs. I'm just phoning about the delivery of our order. First, what about the men's suits.
ORDER CLERK	Yes, the suits will certainly be ready in March.
KLINE	Good, and what about the sports jackets?
ORDER CLERK	They may be ready in March too. But, at this stage we're not certain. We'll be able to give you a definite answer next month.
KLINE	OK, how about the dresses?
ORDER CLERK	They should be delivered in June.
KLINE	Right, then there's the ladies' sweaters?
ORDER CLERK	It depends on the mill, but you could get them next month.
KLINE	That would be fine. We're running very short of swimsuits and what with the spring season approaching, we're keen to know what the position there is. Will they be ready in March?
ORDER CLERK	I'm afraid that's unlikely. But we'll probably manage them in April.
KLINE	Lastly, how are the skirts coming along? You said that we'd have them next month.
ORDER CLERK	I'm sorry, there's not much chance of that but they'll definitely be ready in March.
KLINE	OK, that's fine for now. We'll no doubt be in touch again soon. Bye.
ORDER CLERK	Bye, Mr Kline.

COMPLETED TABLE

	February	March	April	May	June
Men's suits		**			
Sports jackets		?			
Dresses					*
Ladies' sweaters	?				
Swimsuits		X	*		
Skirts	X	**			

121

3 Controlled Practice

2 However, it is unlikely to...

3 In February, we may/might/could...

4 In March, there's not much chance of...

5 In April, the company will certainly/definitely...

6 and we may/might/could...

7 In May the company should/will probably/is likely to...

8 and we may/might/could...

9 In June production will certainly/definitely...

10 but there's not much chance of...

---

4 Transfer

Student B

Use the following information to respond to Student A's questions about delivery dates.

You can say things like:

The Ford Taunus saloons may be delivered in three months time.

They will certainly be ready in six months time.

You'll probably get them in about four or five months from now.

MODEL	DELIVERY DATES	
Ford Taunus 1600 saloons	Minimum 3 months	Maximum 6 months
Ford Granada 2000 saloons	Minimum 2 months	Maximum 5 months
Ford Fiesta 1100 saloons	Minimum 1 month	Maximum 3 months
Ford Escort estate cars	Minimum 2 months (for orders up to 5 vehicles) Minimum 4 months (5 + vehicles)	Maximum 4 months (⟶ 5 vehicles) Maximum 6 months (5 + vehicles)
Ford Transit vans	Minimum 3 months (⟶ 5 vehicles) Minimum 6 months (5 + vehicles)	Maximum 5 months (⟶ 5 vehicles) Maximum 8 months (5 + vehicles)

Unit 28 Sales

1 Listening

TAPESCRIPT

I'd like to begin by taking a look at the differences between our forecast and actual sales figures for last year.

As you can see, for tennis equipment, our actual sales figures were exactly the same as forecast. Our squash and badminton sales were almost as forecast, just £5,000 lower at £180,000. Unlike our sales in these two sectors, there was a big difference in the golf equipment sales... in fact we only achieved £50,000 in total sales. Actual sales again differed from the forecast in our winter sports range... £20,000 lower than expected. In the football equipment sector, there was only a slight variance, just £10,000 lower than forecast. Lastly, as forecast, we reached £25,000 sales in our new market, hang-gliders.

COMPLETED TABLE

Products	Forecast sales	Actual sales
Tennis equipment	£450,000	£450,000
Squash and badminton	£185,000	£180,000
Golf equipment	£100,000	£50,000
Winter sports	£250,000	£230,000
Football	£110,000	£100,000
Hang-gliding	£25,000	£25,000

3 Controlled Practice

1 Actual sales of tennis equipment were exactly (the same) as forecast.

2 Actual squash and badminton sales were almost (the same) as forecast.

3 In the golf equipment sector, as in the winter sports sector, there was a big difference (or variance) between actual and forecast sales.

4 Football sales, like those of squash and badminton equipment, were almost (the same) as forecast.

5 Sales of hang-gliding equipment, unlike golf equipment, were exactly (the same) as forecast.

6 As forecast, sales of tennis equipment reached £450,000.

7 Golf equipment sales, like winter sports sales, did not reach their target.

4 Transfer

Student B
Listen carefully to Student A's presentation of the % tax paid in Molravia and use it to complete Table A below.

TABLE A

Income in US $	% tax
0-2,000	
2,000-3,000	
3,000-5,000	
5,000-10,000	
10,000-20,000	

Now present the information in Table B below to Student A.

The table shows the % tax paid on income earned in Caucasia.

TABLE B

Income in US $	% tax
0-3,000	0
3,000-5,000	20
5,000-7,000	30
7,000-10,000	40
10,000-15,000	50
15,000-20,000	60

Unit 29 Market share developments

1 Listening

TAPESCRIPT

MARKETING MANAGER (EUROPE)	In Europe as a whole, our market share has increased over the last three years from 15% in 77 to 23% in 1979. However, I believe there are some differences in this trend if we look at the three major markets in Europe. Peter, could you tell us about the development in W. Germany?
MARKETING MANAGER (W. GERMANY)	Yes, of course. In West Germany our share has increased, but more slowly. In 77 it stood at 18% and now, in 1979 it is only two points higher. In fact it reached its highest point in 78 at 21%. However, we still made a reasonable profit.
MARKETING MANAGER (EUROPE)	So, we have actually lost ground over the last year. I hope we are going to do better next year. Now, John, what about France?
MARKETING MANAGER (FRANCE)	Our market share in France is now considerably higher than it was in 77. Then it was 12% and it now stands at 28%. So, in fact the trend is even better than the one for Europe as a whole.
MARKETING MANAGER (EUROPE)	Right, let's move on to the UK now. How are things there?
MARKETING MANAGER (UK)	Well, although we are very much in line with general European trends, our market share in 78 was 1 point lower. Otherwise, the figures are the same as for Europe.

COMPLETED TABLE

	W. Germany	France	UK	Europe
1977	18%	12%	15%	15%
1978	21%	22%	18%	19%
1979	20%	28%	23%	23%

3 Controlled Practice

2 *Although* UK market share in 1978 was only 18%, in 1979 it was *three points/somewhat higher than* in W. Germany.

3 French market share in 1977 was only 12%. *However*, in 1979 it was *five points/rather higher than* the figure for Europe as a whole.

4 *Although* UK market share was *one point/slightly lower than* the figure for Europe as a whole in 1978, it was the same in 1977 and 1979.

5 Market share in W. Germany reached 21% in 1978. *However*, in 1979 it was only *20%*.

6 *Although* market share in Europe increased by 8% from 77 to 79, in W. Germany it only increased by *2%*.

7 Between 77 and 78, UK market share increased *more slowly than* French market share.

124

4 Transfer

Student B
Listen to Student A's description of market share development in the car industry in Caucasia. Use the information to draw up the graph below.

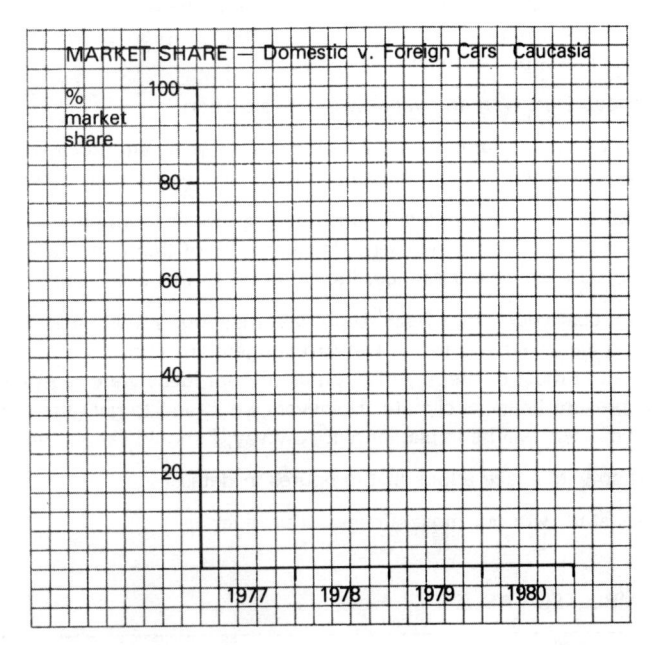

MARKET SHARE — Domestic v. Foreign Cars Caucasia
% market share
(y-axis: 20, 40, 60, 80, 100; x-axis: 1977, 1978, 1979, 1980)

Now use the graph below to describe the development of market share in the car industry in Molravia. Compare and contrast home-produced car sales with foreign-produced car sales. Student A will use the information to draw up a graph.

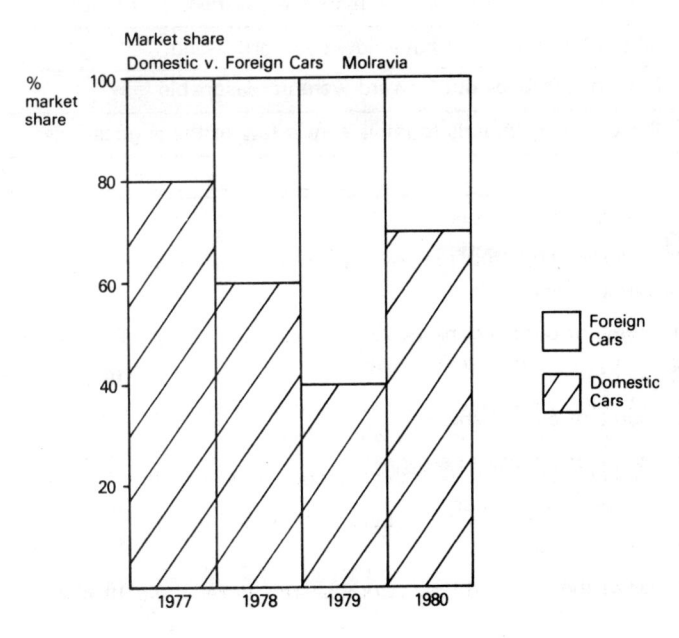

Market share
Domestic v. Foreign Cars   Molravia
% market share
(y-axis: 20, 40, 60, 80, 100; x-axis: 1977, 1978, 1979, 1980)

Foreign Cars
Domestic Cars

Unit 30 End of year report

1 Listening

TAPESCRIPT

Good morning, gentlemen. I want to take a little of your time in this session of the conference to consider the sales of our products over the last year. Unfortunately a few of our sales staff are away on business, but this can't be helped.

But let's start with an overview of the situation.

Most of our products have had a successful year, and none of them have fallen below the sales target. However, some of them have been more successful than others. But more of that later.

As far as our customers are concerned, a few of them have asked us to increase some of our ranges, in particular our coloured pens. However, all of them have expressed satisfaction with the quality of our products and our service. I shall return to this point later.

If you cast your minds back to our last meeting, you'll remember the questionnaires we handed out, in which we asked you to put forward suggestions about our products and services. We have now looked at most of them. Although all of your ideas were reasonable, some of them were unrealistic in the present financial climate. However, we intend to give them further consideration and I am sure a few of them will be implemented. Anyway, I should like to thank all of you for your co-operation.

But now let's take a look at the figures in detail.

We'll start with our most successful product...

COMPLETED TABLE

	TRUE	FALSE
A few of the sales staff did not attend the meeting.	✓	
All of the company's products have had a successful year.		✓
None of the company's products have fallen below the sales target.	✓	
A few of the company's customers have asked for an increased product range.	✓	
Most of the company's customers are satisfied.		✓
All the questionnaires have now been processed.		✓
Most of the ideas put forward were unreasonable.		✓
The company intends to implement a few of the suggestions.	✓	

3 Controlled Practice

Suggested answers are:

1 some of our latest news
2 all of it
3 some of our salesmen
4 some of our sales personnel
5 a few of our customers
6 most of our staff
7 all of them
8 most of them
9 a few of its top managers
10 a lot of our money
11 a lot of time
12 many of our recent meetings
13 none of the strikes
14 a little of the British common sense
15 all of us

GLOSSARY

ACHIEVE	'We achieved sales of £10,000 last month': we reached this figure.
ACTUAL	'Actual sales were lower than forecast': real sales were lower...
ADEQUATE	'The product is adequate': it is OK, but it is not very good.
AGENDA	'There are five points on the agenda today': there are five points to be discussed in the meeting.
ALLOCATE	'We should allocate £5,000 for improvements': we should give £5,000 (out of a budget)... *also* ALLOCATION
ARRANGE	'I have to arrange the accommodation': to book, to organise...
ASSESS	'We need more information before we can assess whether this product will sell': ...before we can decide whether... *also* ASSESSMENT
AXIS	'The years 1960 to 1970 are on the horizontal axis': ...one of the two lines on a graph showing scale.
BACK	'The Managing Director is backing the project': he is supporting it.
BOARD	'There is a meeting of the Board this afternoon': the directors, top executives are meeting...
CANTEEN	'Let's eat in the canteen': ...the place in a factory where meals are served.
CAPITAL	'We need £5,000 capital to begin with': ...sum of money usually for investment or starting a business.
CATER	'The course caters for personnel managers': it is suitable/useful for...
CIF	*abbreviation for* COST, INSURANCE, FREIGHT.
CLIMATE	'It's a very dim economic climate': ...situation, circumstance.
CORE TIME	'Everybody must work between 10 and 4 – this is core time': *see* FLEXITIME.
C.V.	'Please send a full c.v. when you apply for the job': *abbreviation for* CURRICULUM VITAE – details of experience, qualifications etc.
CYCLE	'It's difficult to get out of the cycle of higher costs leading to higher prices': ...a circular system where one event etc. leads to another.
DEAL	'We hope to do a deal with the suppliers': ...to make an arrangement/agreement with...
DEAL WITH	'I have to deal with all the complaints': ...to handle/take action about...
DECLINE	'There has been a decline in profits': ...a drop/fall... *also* TO DECLINE
DIRECT	'John will direct our sales team': ...be in charge of/instruct... *also* DIRECTOR (*eg* SALES DIRECTOR)
DISPATCH	'The goods were dispatched two days ago': they were sent off... *also* DISPATCH DEPARTMENT
DISTRIBUTE	'The cars are distributed by dealers throughout the UK': ...sold in the different parts of the UK. *also* DISTRIBUTOR
DURABLE	'The product is very durable': it will last a long time. *also* DURABILITY
EFFICIENT	'He's very efficient, he'll be difficult to replace': he's good and quick at his job... *also* EFFICIENCY
ENGAGEMENT	'I've got an important engagement today': ...a fixed meeting/appointment.
EQUIVALENT	'The equivalent salary in the UK would be very much lower because of the lower cost of living': the salary paid for doing a similar job...
ESTIMATE	'We estimate that unemployment will rise by one million': we think on the basis of forecasts, calculations etc.... *also* AN ESTIMATE
FIGURES	'The figures are very bad for the first quarter': the financial results...
FILE	'Can you file the tax return under F for finance?': ...put into an ordered storage system... *also* A FILE; FILING (*e.g.* FILING CLERK, DO THE FILING)
FIRM	'He's trying to raise the money to start up his own firm': ...company, business.
FLEXITIME	'We work flexitime': we can vary the (number of) hours we work in any particular day.
IN HAND	'We have £200 cash in hand': ...money readily available.
HANG ON	'Can you hang on while I see if Mr Brown is in his office?': can you wait..(often used on the telephone).
HOLD	'A conference will be held next year': ...will take place, happen...
HOME	'The home market has done well': the domestic/non-foreign market...
IMPLEMENT	'We are going to implement the plan in 1985': put into operation/action.
INFLATION	'The inflation rate has dropped by 2%': rises in prices and wages coupled with a fall in the value of money...
INSTALL	'We are going to install air-conditioning': ...fit, put in...
INSTALMENT	'I pay my mortgage in monthly instalments': ...sums of money paid regularly over a period of time.

INVOICE	'Can you invoice the company direct?': ...send a bill...*also* AN INVOICE
JOB DESCRIPTION	'Before I decide to take the job I'd like to see a full job description': ...details about the responsibilities and functions involved in a particular job.
LEVEL OFF	'Sales have levelled off recently': after increasing/decreasing, sales have remained constant.
MAINTAIN	'We maintained our market share': we kept it at the same level.
MAINTAIN	'The machinery is very expensive to maintain': ...to look after, keep in working order. *also* MAINTENANCE (*e.g.* MAINTENANCE DEPARTMENT)
MANAGE	'He manages the UK business': he is in charge of/is responsible for... *also* MANAGER; MANAGEMENT
MARKET	'We are going to market the new product in Germany': ...to advertise, promote etc....*also* A MARKET (*sometimes* MARKETPLACE); MARKETING
MODEL	'We are going to launch our latest model next month': a new product in a series.
ORDER	'Although this month is quiet, we have plenty of orders next month': ...requests for goods/services...*also* ORDER BOOK
OVERTIME	'Overtime is usually paid at one-and-a-half times normal rates of pay': time worked outside normal working hours...
OVERVIEW	'Before we discuss the matter in detail, I'd like to have an overview': ...a general picture.
PANEL	'I was interviewed by a panel': ...a small group of people. *often* INTERVIEW PANEL
PEAK	'Sales peaked/reached a peak in summer 1975': ...a high point...
PERSONNEL	'We require very highly trained personnel': ...staff/employees.
PREMISES	'We will soon need better premises': ...buildings/offices.
PRESENTATION	'He is giving a presentation of this month's sales': ...a speech/talk about...
R and D	abbreviation for RESEARCH AND DEVELOPMENT.
RANGE	'We have a very wide product range': ...a selection from large to small, expensive to cheap etc.
RATE	'The exchange rate has improved': the relationship between two currencies...
RECRUIT	'We are going to recruit two new members of staff': ...take on/employ... *also* RECRUITMENT (*e.g.* RECRUITMENT PROCEDURE)
REFERENCE	'His old employer gave him a good reference': ...assessment of performance (usually for recruitment purposes).
REPRESENT	'He represents a pharmaceutical company': he is a salesman/promoter for... *also* A REPRESENTATIVE (*often abbreviated to* REP): a salesman.
REPRESENT	'This line represents sales in West Gemany': ...shows/displays...
RESIGN	'We hope he will resign so we won't have to fire him': ...leave his job voluntarily...*also* RESIGNATION
RUN	'This machine is very expensive to run': ...to operate, keep operating. *also* TO RUN SHORT OF: to not have enough of; RUNNING COSTS
SCHEDULE	'I have two meetings scheduled for this afternoon': ...fitted into a timetable... *also* A SCHEDULE
SECTOR	'The industrial sector is expanding': ...defined area of activity/business...
SHARE	'We have a large share of the German market': ...percentage of the market held...*often* MARKET SHARE
STABILISE	'Next year the market should stabilise': become steady, not move up and down.
STOPPAGE	'We can't afford another stoppage to production': ...a breakdown/halt...
SUBSIDIARY	'We have subsidiaries all over the world': ...associated companies owned by a parent company...
SUBSIDISE	'Our foreign operations are subsidising the home market': ...supporting financially...
TAKE OVER	'The financial director is going to take over responsibility for salaries': ...replace someone else as responsible for...*also* A TAKE-OVER: one company buys the majority of shares in another company.
TARGET	'Sales were exactly on target': ...as forecast/planned.
TERMINAL	'The goods are distributed from the terminal': ...a central place where goods arrive or are dispatched.
TERMS	'We haven't agreed on the terms yet': ...the conditions of a contract/agreement.
TRADE FAIR	'I'm attending the trade fair in Zurich': an exhibition of products, services etc.
TREND	'There is a downward trend in sales': ...a general movement...